5001
simple things
to do for others
(and Yourself!)

5001

simple things

to do for others

(and Yourself!)

from your friends at
Liguori Publications

Liguori
LIGUORI, MISSOURI

Imprimi Potest:
Thomas D. Picton, C.Ss.R.
Provincial, Denver Province
The Redemptorists

Published by Liguori Publications
Liguori, Missouri
To order, call 800-325-9521
www.liguori.org

Library of Congress Cataloging-in-Publication Data
On file

Liguori Publications, a nonprofit corporation, is an apostolate of the Redemptorists. To learn more about the Redemptorists, visit Redemptorists.com.

Printed in the United States of America

14 13 12 11 10   5 4 3 2 1
First edition

Contents

Acknowledgments

A great number of people contributed to this book in the hopes that readers would find ways to pay it forward in every way every day.

Rebecca Molen
Richard Potts
Suann Fields
Patricia DeClue
Deborah Meister
Angela Baumann
Maureen Connolly
Wendy Barnes
Regina Competti
Robb Holzrichter
Liz Halfmann
Mike Ramsey
Mathew Kessler
Pat Staten
Lisa Bielicki
Marjorie Kolb
Kim Dolan
Denise Jones
Dianna Graveman
Christopher Miller
Pam Hummelsheim
...and the entire staff of Liguori Publications

All my thanks...
Jay Staten
Editorial Director

Introduction

The concept "pay it forward" is not new. It didn't begin when the movie of the same name blazed to the top of the charts in 2000 or even with *Acts of Kindness: How to Make a Gentle Difference* by Meladee McCarty and Hanoch McCarty (HCI, 1994). Many of us understand it from our early Bible education:

> *"For I was hungry and you gave me food, I was thirsty and you gave me something to drink, I was a stranger and you welcomed me, I was naked and you gave me clothing, I was sick and you took care of me, I was in prison and you visited me." Then the righteous will answer him, "Lord, when was it that we saw you hungry and gave you food, or thirsty and gave you something to drink? And when was it that we saw you a stranger and welcomed you, or naked and gave you clothing? And when was it that we saw you sick or in prison and visited you?" And the king will answer them, "Truly I tell you, just as you did it to one of the least of these who are members of my family, you did it to me."*
>
> Matthew 25:35–40

Mother Teresa quoted these passages often and lived her life believing that everyone is Jesus in disguise. She dedicated her life to missioning to the poorest and most abandoned.

A little trick to living the words of Matthew—every time you see the word *you* in the passage, insert your name.

In the following pages, you will find many simple suggestions for taking advantage of a moment to make tomorrow a better place, for seeing opportunities to act and to give

This philosophy is also about making small improvements to ourselves. As we improve our own lives, we improve the lives of those around us. We become better friends, better partners, better parents, better neighbors, and better citizens of this planet

Your Friends at
Liguori Publications

Kindness, like a boomerang, always returns

—Anonymous

Simple Ways to Start Paying It Forward

The concept is simple: a) turn the focus away from ourselves; b) center on given rather than taking, and c) experience joy on both sides.

1. Leave a copy of a really great book you've read in a café or airplane for someone else to enjoy

2. Say something nice or funny or goofy to the toll-booth attendant

3. Put a quarter in a meter—any meter—that's about to expire

4. Forgive the driver directing a little road rage your way

5. Buy lunch/dinner for someone homeless on the street

6. Offer to do *pro bono* work on a project where your skills are needed

7. Mentor someone

8. Make donations—often

9. Give the shirt off your back (or coat)

10. Say a prayer when you hear a siren—there is usually a victim behind it

11. Compliment a stranger

12. Tip those in the service industry

13. Give directions when asked

14. Send a box of donuts or bagels to a fire station or construction site

15. Show respect equally to *all* human beings

16. Teach kids something you wish you had known at their age

17. Spend time with someone who is terminally ill

18. Help a pregnant woman

19. Sit and talk with a homeless person and learn his or her story

20. Lend something to someone and forget about the debt

21. Volunteer at a battered-women's shelter

22. Let someone cut in front of you

23. When leaving a foreign country, give leftover currency to a resident

24. Hold the door open

25. Put a tip (as generous as possible) in a street musician's jar and say thanks for the entertainment

26. Help someone carry bags

27. Give local tips to tourists

28. Give someone the benefit of the doubt

29. Encourage someone to pursue a dream

30. Offer the delivery person a cold drink on a hot day

31. Offer the delivery person a hot drink on a cold day

32. Show respect and give thanks to a soldier regardless of your personal politics

33. Replace an angry or bitter thought with a loving one

34. Give yourself (blood, time, talents, brawn)

35. Be hands-on

36. Fight for what you believe in

37. Contribute to a friend's children's education fund

38. Give up your seat to someone who needs it more

39. Listen to others' opinions without interruption and consider their argument thoughtfully

40. Accept that you are able to control only *your* actions and responses

41. Take responsibility for your actions in all things

42. Stop to consider the consequences of your actions

43. Lead by example

44. Give others a chance to prove themselves and their abilities

45. Be the first to volunteer for an unpleasant, messy task

46. Carefully consider what your wants and needs truly are

47. Be willing to fail before quitting

48. Be alive and aware of everything around you

49. Don't let the world desensitize you

50. Accept your personal flaws and those of others

51. Remember the environment

52. Understand that aging is natural and happens to all of us

53. True communities share the burdens of all members

54. Money does far more good in the hands of many than in the hands of a few

55. Say please and thank you everywhere

Character Traits of Givers

56. Promote adaptability

57. Support an appreciation for people

58. Stay attentive

59. Are available

60. Reinforce their commitment daily

61. Keep their compassion

62. Place their concern where it will do the most good

63. Show confidence

64. Are always considerate

65. Understand that consistency wins the game

66. Find contentment in what they can accomplish

67. Promote cooperation

68. Fortify their courage

69. Keep creativity flowing

70. Stay decisive

71. Encourage deference

72. Are known for their dependability

73. Stay determined

74. Show they are always diligent

75. Exercise discernment and discretion

76. Know that efficiency allows you to accomplish more

77. Understand that equality keeps the balance

78. Are always fair

79. Are faithful

80. Practice fearlessness

81. Remain flexibility

82. Understand forgiveness

83. Know that winners are friendly

84. Realize that generosity with time and resources will make them rich

85. Are known for your gentleness

86. Express their gratitude

87. Remain honest

88. Are humble before god

89. Know the worth of their integrity

90. Celebrate joyfulness

91. Practice kindness

92. Indulge in love

93. Are loyal to their values

94. Understand we are all meek on the inside

95. Believe God is merciful—we just try to follow his example

96. Observe what is truth

97. Keep their optimism

98. Are patient

99. Practice prudence

100. Are known for their punctuality

101. Promote their purpose

102. Are always resourceful

103. Respect those around them and those who seek their help

104. Know we are all responsible for humankind

105. Practice self-control

106. Don't let their sincerity overrule logic

107. Are submissive before God

108. Remain tactful

109. Are thorough

110. Believe thriftiness will pay off

111. Know the world is in need of tolerance

112. Are trustworthy

113. Always promote the truth

114. Understand that we can't live on virtue alone, but we can't live without it

Every Day in Every Way

115. Consider how your actions impact others

116. Taking care of yourself is as important as taking care of others

117. Participate in life—at work, at home, with your children, your family, and in your community

118. Meet everyone you pass with a smile and a "good day!" Make it a game (and make yourself smile) to see how many return the smiles

119. Take a few minutes to do a mental check of your physical and mental health and your attitude

120. Check the physical and mental health of your family

121. Check your "to do" list—someone is waiting for you to do something

122. Don't keep others waiting

123. Exercise

124. Eat breakfast

125. Dress according to your needs for the day

126. Take extra time with your appearance

127. When you look good, you feel good

128. Live the entire day as if the glass were half full

129. Take five minutes at midday to stretch your body and reassess your day

130. Laugh—a lot!

131. Practice good time-management skills

132. Acknowledge those who work in the service industries— smile and say thank you

133. Talk to your letter carrier, thank him/her for delivering your mail

134. Tell your family—children, spouse, siblings, parents, etc.—you love them

135. Forgive someone—let go of old hurt

136. Forgive yourself!

137. Pray and meditate every day—clears your mind, clears your soul, and gets you moving

138. Give someone the benefit of the doubt

139. Hold the door open

140. Stay in touch with the world—get the news (Internet, paper, television, etc.)

141. Answer questions

142. Return calls

143. Respond to e-mails

144. Communicate with friends and family—even if it's a simple email

145. Say thank you to someone who helps you

146. Compliment at least one person every day without fail

147. Think positive—look for the good in every situation

148. Say a little prayer asking God's protection when you leave home or work

149. Stop being afraid, let go of your ego

150. Silence is golden. Resist the urge to chime in when someone is sharing an experience that is new to them and old to you

151. Focus on listening

152. Listen to what people are saying. Ask questions to affirm that you have heard what they've said

153. Be courteous to other workers—remember this is their job and that is how they put food on their table

154. Give a friend a hug

155. Once a day stop to smell the roses, look at the sky, and thank God for your time alive

156. Count your blessings

157. Question your expectations of yourself and of others

158. Cultivate grace

159. Keep the sense of wonder alive

160. Practice self-restraint

161. Practice leadership

162. Provoke excellence in yourself and others

163. Swallow your pride

164. Learn a new word every day

165. Dance to your own tune

166. Indulge in one great fantasy

167. Be grateful for all the people who share your day

168. See your commitments through

169. Take time to learn something new every day—you never know when that knowledge will come in handy and help someone else

170. Before you go to sleep, think about one thing you learned today about your family, friends, and coworkers

171. Power down thirty minutes before you go to sleep. Turn off the tv, the computer, the iPod, and the phone and just relax

Driving Happiness Home

172. Keep yourself, your family, and the community safe

173. Think before you drive

174. Before starting your car, make sure children are snugly fastened into their safety seats and harnesses

175. Don't talk on your cell phone, text message, adjust your radio, or play with other electronics while you are driving

176. Let someone switch lanes in front of you

177. Obey the law concerning speeds, seat belts, etc.

178. Make sure your car is in good working order and tires are properly inflated—a safe car adds to the safety of others

179. Remember that the person going slowly in front of you may be a 16-year-old just learning how to drive, so don't honk, speed around them, etc.

180. Remember that the person going slowly in front of you may be an elderly driver with delayed reaction time

181. Don't empty your trash, dirty diapers, fast food refuse, or ash tray on the side of the road or in a parking lot. Find a trash can at a gas station or convenience store and dispose of it properly

182. If you see someone broken down or with a flat tire on the side of the road, call the police on your cell phone

183. Help conserve energy and keep the air quality high by maintaining your vehicle and following the speed limit

184. Donate child car seats and booster seats you no longer need to a nonprofit organization that gives them to parents who can't afford them

185. Don't express road rage—it's dangerous, and if you have passengers in the car, they don't need to hear your ranting and raving!

186. Never take up two parking spaces in a parking lot. Back out and try again or park far away where there are plenty of spaces

187. Never block someone else when parking

188. If you ding the car next to you, take a photo of it with your phone and put a note with your contact information on the windshield. The photo will protect you if the person claims it was a lot worse than it really was

189. Don't be a looky-loo. When you pass an accident, obey those handling traffic and keep moving

190. If you see an accident happen, call 911 (or your state's highway emergency number). Stick around to give a statement to the police

191. Take a first-aid class

Parking Lot Practices

192. Easy exercise—park as far as possible from the entrance and add steps to your trip

193. If you park at the far end of the lot, save some steps for the shopping-cart crew by bringing in stray carts

194. Keep a pad of sticky notes in your car and leave anonymous messages of kindness on the windshield of your parking lot neighbors

195. Pay for someone's valet parking

196. In a standoff for a parking space, let the other driver have it

197. Don't park so close to the car next to you that the other person has to crawl in from the other side (or ding your door to open his)

198. Help someone pack groceries into their car—mother with cranky kids, older person, someone who looks tired

199. Collect the change you find while walking in the parking lot and give it to the next homeless person you see

Super Nice at the Supermarket

200. If you put something in your grocery cart and then two aisles later decide you don't want it, don't just put it on any shelf. Either take it back to the correct spot or give it to the cashier when you check out

201. Compliment the cashier and the bagger on a job well done

202. Many stores have comment cards. If an employee does something special for you, write it all down on the comment card and send it in

203. If you're tall and you see someone having difficulty reaching an item on a high shelf, offer to help

204. Help the parent who is shopping with the screaming child(ren)—ask if there is anything you can do to help, let them go in front of you at cash register, etc.

205. When you drop something—pick it up. If your child drops something—pick it up

206. If it breaks, leaks, etc., tell a worker immediately—don't just walk away

207. Say please and thank you to the employees. If they say hello, say it back

208. Tell the cashier if an item rings up at the wrong price—even if it's in your favor

209. Leave coupons you don't need on the shelf with the item for someone who can use it

210. When you pull a cart out of the rack, offer it to the person waiting behind you

211. After you've loaded your groceries into your car, put your cart in the grocery-cart corral instead of leaving it in the middle of the lot

212. Use in-store hand sanitizers

Gym Gems

213. Be a good workout neighbor—wipe the equipment after you use it

214. Put hand weights, dumbbells, etc., back in their appropriate place after using—don't make someone go looking for the weights they need

215. Help someone who is having trouble—show them how to use a machine, offer to spot them, etc.

216. Don't sing along with the songs you may be hearing on your ear buds or head phones—no one wants to hear you sing!

217. You start to recognize the other people who are working out at the same time you are—tell someone when you notice they've lost weight!

218. Don't hog machines

219. Let someone who is doing exercises on machines in a circuit use your machine—they'll be on and off quickly and will appreciate your act of kindness very much

220. Don't reserve a machine by leaving your water bottle, book, towel, etc., on it

221. Use machines appropriately—don't bang the weights, use the wrong weights, etc.

222. Rerack the weight plates when you're finished using a machine—don't just leave them for the next person to put away

Love Thy Neighbor

223. If your neighbor is infirm, toss his newspaper up to the front door so it's easier to get

224. When a neighbor is going to be away, offer to collect the mail and newspaper

225. When a neighbor is going to be away, offer to feed pets

226. When a neighbor is going to be away, offer to water her lawn

227. When a neighbor is going to be away, offer to mow her lawn

228. Clean out the gutters of an elderly or infirm neighbor's house

229. When you pay your water bill, pay an elderly or poor neighbor's bill too

230. Help a neighbor who is bothered by telemarketing calls to register for the no-call list, install an answering machine, and use caller ID

231. Help an older friend, neighbor, or family member develop a new resumé, prepare for an interview, or create an e-mail account to post a resumé

232. Rake your neighbor's leaves and dispose of them properly

233. Conduct a local walking audit of your neighborhood and notify the appropriate agencies if you see missing street signs, potholes, common-property damage, or dangerous conditions

234. Offer to walk your neighbor's dog if he cannot

235. Organize a neighborhood walk-to-school group to accompany neighborhood children to school one day a week

236. If you see a lost dog, take it in and try to find the owner

237. If you see an owner trying to find a lost dog, help her put up signs, drive around the neighborhood, etc.

238. In an emergency, drive or go with your neighbor to the hospital, babysit his children, or clean up the mess so she doesn't have to when she gets home

239. Set up a computer for a neighbor who is not computer savvy

240. When you see your neighbor struggling to do jobs without the proper ladder, tools, etc. offer to lend them yours

241. On Veterans Day, put little American flags in the yard of a neighbor who is a veteran

242. Get into the habit of picking up broken bottles and other trash from the sidewalks around your house and in your neighborhood

243. Pick up after your dog

244. Obey subdivision rules

245. Don't have loud parties late at night

246. Keep your dogs quiet

247. If the neighbor kid is trying to earn some money by raking leaves, mowing lawns, getting the newspaper while you are on vacation—hire the kid

248. Say hello to the neighbors you see when walking around the neighborhood

249. As a neighborhood, collect teddy bears for police officers to give to traumatized children. Attach a note to each teddy bear for the donating resident to sign

250. Keep an eye on children who play near your home—make sure they are playing safely or tell them to stop and go somewhere else to play

251. If kids get their ball or Frisbee stuck in a tree or in a big puddle—help them retrieve it

252. Keep your yard and home nice so it doesn't bring down the property values of the neighboring homes

253. Let your neighbors know ahead of time if you're going to have a party and that people will be parking up and down the street

254. Make sure your guests don't block driveways or block the way in or out of the neighborhood

255. Make sure party guests stay off your neighbors' property and don't leave beverage containers or other trash outside

256. If your neighbor leaves his garage door open, let him know in case he simply forgot to close it

257. If your neighbor has a death in the family, let her know you care by bringing her stationery supplies

258. After the funeral is over and the commotion dies down, stop over with continued support, offer to bring a meal, help him go through his loved one's things, ask him to accompany you as you run errands just to get out of the house, etc.

259. Organize spring and fall clean-up projects. Choose an area that needs attention and collect debris, abandoned items, and other materials that have collected in the area. Collect money to rent a dumpster for the community to use for a day

260. Get a group of neighbors together and take the free classes at home-improvement stores so you can help each other with home repairs

261. Organize a neighborhood garage sale. The more families that participate, the more people will come

262. Donate a percentage of the community garage-sale money to a charity or neighborhood project or party

263. It's OK to be your neighbor's keeper—watch their house and property while they are away and report any trespassers

264. Watch out for the neighborhood kids—if you see them speeding, drinking, smoking, doing drugs, etc., tell their parents

265. If you have a basement and live in a tornado-prone area, make sure your basementless neighbors know they are welcome to seek shelter there

266. Roll an elderly neighbor's garbage cans back up the driveway at the end of trash pick-up day

267. If the wind blows a neighbor's trash can into the street, retrieve them

268. Gather a few neighbors to adopt an entrance to your neighborhood and periodically have a get-together to keep it weeded and cleaned up

269. Bring refreshments to the clean-up and make it a party!

270. Offer to tutor a neighborhood child for free

271. Anonymously leave a bouquet of flowers on a neighbor's front porch

272. When a neighbor is moving, offer to help

273. Take snacks to friends helping the neighbor move

274. Watch the neighbor's kids and/or pets so they don't get in the movers' way

275. When going to the farmer's market or produce stand, buy your neighbor something special that he might not buy for himself

Love Thy Neighbor(hood)

276. Organize a block party based on a theme such as "neighborhood clean-up," "crime watch," or to raise funds for a charity

277. In mid March, plant marigold seeds in small pots. Deliver them to your neighbors' doorsteps for May Day (May 1st). Herbs are also nice—especially basil and rosemary

278. Organize a community garden—fresh veggies for everyone! Consider making a pact with neighbors to donate half the produce to the local food bank

279. Start a neighborhood-watch group—your local police can help

280. Plant flowers throughout the neighborhood

281. Form a group to welcome newcomers with a bread basket and list of neighborhood resources (police/fire numbers, local barber/beauty shop names, veterinarian contact, etc.)

282. Volunteer to be the webmaster for a neighborhood blog site or website and encourage everyone to share their news, things for sale, things being given away, how they need help, beautification ideas, etc.

283. Find out if you have neighbors that are unable to drive or get a ride to vote and arrange to take them with you when you vote

284. Sit and visit with someone in your neighborhood who has no family close by

285. Talk to your letter carrier—say thank you for delivering your mail

286. Start a work pool for elderly neighbors (or others in need)—spring clean-up, simple house repairs, simple errands (such as transportation to the doctor's office)

287. Organize kids' play time, taking turns with parental supervision, thus allowing all parents a little downtime to take care of chores, errands, or just relax

288. Have students from a high school or youth group put on a Vacation Bible School for area children, especially in the inner city where churches may lack the room in their own facilities

289. Fight to keep local parks drug-free and litter-free

290. Fight to keep the local playground and swimming pool open

291. Organize a neighborhood meeting and discuss the special needs of children in your area

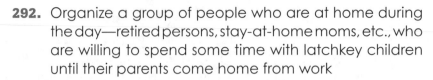

292. Organize a group of people who are at home during the day—retired persons, stay-at-home moms, etc., who are willing to spend some time with latchkey children until their parents come home from work

293. Start a neighborhood reading group

294. Invite the fire department to teach a group of neighbors basic first aid and CPR

295. Report suspected child or spousal abuse

296. Report suspected criminal activities

297. Start a neighborhood Christmas tradition similar to the Mexican tradition *posadas* (going from house to house each evening). It's a great way to meet new people and share the holiday spirit

298. Collect unused gym equipment from the neighbors and start a neighborhood gym in someone's garage

299. Stay abreast of all upcoming community initiatives and their impact on your neighborhood

300. Start a neighborhood e-newsletter

301. Organize a neighborhood check-in project for seniors or people who are ill or disabled. Each person takes two names and calls at a specific time each morning and evening "just to check in." If someone doesn't answer after three tries in a 45-minute period, check on her in person

302. Decorate the neighborhood (or building) for the holidays

303. Run for local commissioner

304. Help out in a school lunchroom, classroom, or gym

305. Get to know the police officers who patrol your neighborhood

306. Be a secret Santa to people who are alone during the holidays

307. Purchase painted-lady caterpillars and a butterfly house. Invite neighborhood children to stop by daily to observe the caterpillars as they spin a cocoon, hatch, and become butterflies. When they're ready, release the butterflies outdoors

308. If you or someone you know is getting married, consider a live butterfly release as an eco-friendly and beautiful alternative to tossing rice, blowing bubbles, or releasing balloons

309. Organize a neighborhood picnic—but take it to the local firehouse so the firefighters can join in

310. Schedule a block party for no reason

311. Frequent small businesses in your area and if you honestly can, talk them up and recommend them to your friends

312. Don't burn yard debris when children are playing outside

313. Get neighbors to commit land to a wildlife habitat

Make the World a Better Place— One Good Deed at a Time

314. Collect food donations at work and deliver them to a food pantry

315. Offer to be a "foster parent" for animal rescue organizations

316. Collect old towels and other things for the nonprofit animal-rescue shelter in your area needs

317. If you notice a library book has been misshelved—put it where it belongs

318. If you notice clothes that have fallen off hangers in a store while you go through the racks—hang them up

319. Don't leave the clothes you don't want in the dressing room of a store—bring them out and either give them to the sales person or hang them back up

320. Volunteer to help at your child's school—be a reader for a class, grade papers at night for a teacher, be a teacher's aide, etc.

321. Smile at those you meet on the street

322. Volunteer to be a scout leader, teach junior achievement, chaperone your children's field trip, etc.

323. Do two good deeds at once: Recycle your aluminum cans, paper, and ink cartridges by donating them to a church or school

324. Cut the plastic rings that hold soda cans together so they don't get stuck around a bird's neck

325. Let the person who really needs to go the bathroom—a child, mother who needs to change a diaper—in front of you in the bathroom

326. If you don't want to talk to telemarketers, register for the do-not-call list, screen your calls, or politely say "No thanks" and hang up, but don't be rude—they're just trying to make a living

327. Give up your seat to an elderly person, pregnant woman, disabled person, or person with small children

328. Don't sit right in front of people—especially kids—at a movie theater, event, etc. that isn't stadium seating

329. Clear your table at a fast-food restaurant—don't leave your mess behind

330. Cover your mouth with the crook of your arm when you cough or sneeze!

331. Instead of buying presents for people who really don't need anything, donate the money to an organization such as the St. Vincent de Paul Society, which helps people in your own city, or Heifer International, which helps people around the world

332. Pay for the lunch of the table across the room

333. Hold an umbrella over someone without one when it's raining—parent with small child, elderly person, person on crutches, etc.

334. Buy extra umbrellas at a dollar store, keep them in your car, and hand them to homeless people, the Salvation Army bell ringer, and people waiting at a bus stop or walking down the street

335. Keep inexpensive gloves and hats in your car and keep them in your car, and hand them to homeless people, the Salvation Army bell ringer, and people waiting at a bus stop or walking down the street

336. When you tell someone you will say a prayer for him—do it

337. Say a prayer for someone without telling her

338. Believe in the power of prayer

339. Open the door for someone

340. Give your unwanted DVDs and CDs to a children's hospital or nursing home for movie night

341. If you get a voicemail message from someone who clearly dialed the wrong number, call him back and tell him so he can try again

342. When someone confides in you about a problem, make a note to reminding yourself to ask again in a couple of weeks

343. Ask before you pet a stranger's dog

344. Donate to the Rescue Dog Association

345. Send a thank you card to your local volunteer fire department

346. Hold the elevator door open when you see people running for it

347. Write to one social-justice organizer or leader each month just to encourage them

348. Fight to stop religious persecution

349. Let a child push the button in your elevator car—it will make her and her parent very happy

350. When someone has done something nice for you, accept the good deed with gratitude and thank you

351. Adopt a pet from a shelter—and have it spayed or neutered

352. Go through the thrift store and randomly drop dollar bills in pockets of clothing being sold

353. Give money to a shelter to help cover the costs of spaying and neutering

354. If the service in a restaurant, business, etc. was great, call a manager over and tell the manager in front of the employee, or write a glowing compliment on a comment card and send it to corporate headquarters

355. Smile and say something nice to people you see up close for a brief amount of time—the toll-booth worker, the fast-food worker, the trash collector, etc.

356. Donate soda tabs to the Ronald McDonald House or other organization that collects them

357. Invite a single, pregnant woman to live with your family

358. Throw a birthday party for someone on probation

359. Always send thank you notes

360. Leave a random tip for someone who's cleaning the streets or a public restroom

361. Donate your business clothes that no longer fit to an organization that helps underprivileged people get interviews and jobs

362. Donate the jackets and coats your children have outgrown or you will never wear again to a clothing drive

363. Organize a prayer vigil for peace

364. Send an unexpected greeting card to someone who needs a little lift

365. Teach your children about community responsibility by taking them along when you visit a friend in the hospital or retirement home

366. Write one CEO a month to affirm or critique the ethics of her company

367. When you upgrade your cell phone, donate the old phone to an organization who gives them to the poor. They can use them to make 911 calls, which are free

368. Fast in empathy with the 2 billion people who live on less than a dollar a day

369. Connect with a group of migrant workers or farmers who grow your food and visit their farm. Pick some vegetables with them

Growing Family Ties

370. Each day tell your family you love them

371. Make communication with your immediate and distant family members a habit—email is perfect when time and distance are an issue

372. Don't forget the human touch—hug each other often

373. Practice positive parenting—kids learn by example

374. Pray for your family—not just those in need

375. Thank the elders of the family for the guidance and experience they bring to your life

376. Learn to forgive and love again

377. Read to the children in the family as often as possible

378. Have older children read to you—it deepens your bond and helps them learn

379. Read to the elders of your family who can no longer easily read—could be news, stories of interest, or fiction

380. Listen, without being judgmental, to close and distant family

381. Don't get tied up in spats within the family

382. Remember to compliment family members

383. Remember to thank family members

384. Let your sister borrow your favorite outfit

385. Write a family cookbook—get all generations to contribute recipes

386. Teach a teen to be a good driver

387. Turn off the television one night a week and interact with family

388. Host a family holiday

389. Set a lunch date with a sibling, cousin, aunt, uncle, etc., just to catch up

390. Set a regular lunch date with your spouse

391. Call your parents to apologize for being a brat when you were a child (especially if you have kids now)

392. Give your parents a coupon for a day of your time to do anything around the house

393. Thank your parents for how they raised you

394. Call your parents just to say hi

395. Start a family e-newsletter

396. Send your parents flowers on your birthday

397. Put an ad in the announcement section of the paper, awarding your parents the "Parents of the Year" award

398. Leave your parents a voicemail singing your favorite childhood song

399. Play football in the house (with a Nerf ball)

400. Play tickle monster with the kids—even when they are "too old"

401. Hold and participate in family meetings

402. Start a family college fund not just for your own kids, but for other kids in the family who need the help

403. Plant a fruit tree every time a new baby is born in the family—when it begins to produce fruit, donate it to a food pantry

404. Plant an evergreen when a family member dies

405. Write thank you notes to family members

406. Tuck love notes in your spouse's purse, briefcase, or lunch box

407. Write notes of encouragement on stickers and put on children's mirrors so they see them first thing in the morning

408. Dads, plan together time with your teenage daughter—go where she wants to go and listen to what she wants to say

409. Moms, do the same with your sons

410. Plan one-on-one time each week with each of your children or grandchildren

411. Godparents, keep a relationship with that child throughout their life

412. Educate children in the family about the family history

413. Encourage family members to develop their personal talents

414. Do your least favorite family chore without being asked or complaining...then don't tell anyone

415. Take a spontaneous road trip with a sister, brother, cousin

416. Take a family road trip with no DVD

417. Take your siblings out for ice cream—no matter their age

418. Plan regular family movie and game nights

419. Respect differences of opinion within the family

420. Organize family volunteer campaigns

421. Choose a family charity. Include cousins and other distant relatives and donate together

422. Send birthday cards, holiday cards, and congratulations notes

423. Make a family calendar with important dates—anniversaries, birthdays, graduations—and be sure to call or e-mail on those dates

424. Create a family website to share photos and notes. Give the user name and passwords to everyone so they can add their own photos and notes

425. Organize a family clean-up and repair day for elderly members of the family

426. Take the time and be willing to travel to be with a family member in need

427. Stop making excuses for not being involved in your family's lives

428. Remember family members overseas—make sure they know you care

429. Send goody packages to family members on military deployment

430. Keep up on family news

431. Organize a tutor group within the family. Even distant members can tutor via the Internet

432. Encourage education

433. Promote good mental and physical health for all ages

434. Plant a family garden. Give excess food to a local food pantry or soup kitchen

435. Volunteer as a family in a soup kitchen on holidays

436. Create a family scholarship in the name of a deceased member

437. At Christmas, have a family *posada*. Each night visit one residence for the nine days leading up to Christmas Eve

438. Have a family reunion at least once a year

439. Have a family yard sale and donate the money to the family college fund

440. Read bedtime stories for the young and the young at heart—remember you can do this over the web for distant relatives

441. Share meals. Pot lucks make great get-togethers

442. Start a health challenge with siblings and cousins—exercise, eat right, and lose weight. Be sure to award prizes

443. Have a family blessing at least once a year

444. Regularly visit family in nursing homes—make sure the staff knows you are family and you care

445. Take older family members on a drive—see the country, see Christmas lights, visit the family cemetery

446. Remember the departed with flowers at the grave regularly

447. Organize a family team for a walkathon

448. Take classes together

449. Forgive insults and avoid family drama

450. Include "family" not related by blood/marriage in family activities

451. Take the time to appreciate the talents and gifts of each family member and how those gifts better the world

452. Teach children responsibility to family, to themselves, and to community

453. Learn first aid together

454. Instead of giving gifts, give experiences—they create memories that last far longer than any tangible gift

455. Mourn losses together as family

456. Talk to younger family members about their future plans, give advice, or do research

457. Take regular family portraits

458. Don't be afraid to recognize family problems—depression, abuse, addiction within the family. Use family pressure or intervention to seek help for the person

459. Recognize that there may be a family in need within your own extended family. Adopt them for the holidays—food, clothing, necessities, and presents for the kids

460. Start a family-sponsored little league team in your home town

461. Adopt a school in the name of the family and provide support through time, energy, and money

462. Schedule various family members to provide meals and other support services for family members with new babies or recovering from illness

463. Update your will, medical directives, and power of attorney

464. Talk to each family member or hold a family meeting to talk about what's in your will, medical directives, and power of attorney so everyone is aware of everyone else's intentions

465. Make arrangements and pay for your own funeral

466. Question family values and expectations—are they still right for future generations?

467. Use frequent-flyer miles to get college kids or military home for holidays

468. Create your own unique family mission statement

469. Balance your work and your family life. Help others in the family do the same

470. Don't let "urgent" matters replace "important" matters in your family life

471. Remember that as part of a family and/or marriage, you are in this for the long haul

472. Cultivate spirituality in the family

473. Identify challenges within the family and work with each other to deal with them

474. Plan for tomorrow—physically, mentally, and financially

475. Respect individuality among family members

476. Remember that all members of the family are responsible for their own actions and are entitled to their own opinions

477. Say what you mean and mean what you say

478. Don't be a slave to family expectations, and don't expect others to be, either

479. Reach out to family members for coaching and feedback

480. Incorporate your commitments and your family priorities

Capture Your History

481. Recording thoughts, events, and the general everyday things, helps future generations understand part of their own history

482. Keep a journal. You don't have to write every day, but keep track of important things

483. Create scrapbooks for your family and friends to record important occasions as well as simple moments

484. Create a family tree. Document births, adoptions, marriages, deaths, etc.

485. Organize family heirlooms and label them for future reference

486. Label your quilts and volunteer to label those of others: Write quilt maker, year, and any other information on a label and sew it to the back bottom corner of quilt

487. Preserve family documents such as family Bibles, old homestead claims, military papers, immigration and citizenship papers, journals

488. Visit the StoryCorps website to find out how to record the oral history of your family (www.storycorps.org/record-your-story/)

489. Capture your ethnic background

490. Learn where your mother's family came from

491. Learn where your father's family come from

492. Make plans to join with family members to visit the old country

493. List your family traditions

494. Record the classic jokes in the family

495. Record the favorite family songs

496. Write down thoughts on what it was like to grow up

497. Write about family friends

498. Record the nicknames of every family member

499. Write a story about the perfect day with the family

500. Share family photos through the wonders of digital technology

501. Take old family film footage, edit it into a story, and give copies to everyone

502. Create a family contact list, including cousins, nieces and nephews, godchildren—everyone associated with the family. Then contact them

503. Visit the old country or old family farm, record the experience, and share with other family members

504. Study your cultural heritage

505. When creating the family genealogy, don't forget to include important history events and locations—our lives are impacted by the experiences of those around us

Care and Feeding of Tomorrow's Adults

506. Work with your spouse on what is important in raising children

507. Include the extended family in the child-rearing process

508. Develop ways to provide positive family communications

509. Encourage healthy relationships with adults and other family members

510. Work with neighbors to create a kid-friendly environment

511. Remember that schools do not raise your children, you do

512. Make sure school is a "growth" environment where your kids can explore and learn

513. Be involved with your child's schooling and school

514. Cook with your family

515. Assign household chores to everyone and teach that by doing these chores, we each contribute to the good of the whole

516. Establish and enforce family boundaries

517. Teach your children school boundaries

518. Work with other parents in the neighborhood to establish neighborhood boundaries

519. Raise children to understand they are part of a wider community

520. Be a good role model for your children

521. Remember all kids need adult role models outside family

522. Understand the ramifications of peer influence

523. Let your children know you have high expectations for them

524. Create, participate, and sign children up for creative activities

525. Sign kids up for youth programs in the community

526. Raise children to understand they are part of the church community

527. Empower kids to make good decisions

528. Motivate your children to achieve whatever they set out to do

529. Teach children to set goals for themselves

530. Assign tasks to each child that contribute to the overall good of the family

531. Eat dinner together and find out what is going on in their lives

532. Ask, what did you learn today?

533. Enforce homework rules

534. Pay attention to what they're saying by looking them in the eye

535. Eat ice cream for dinner

536. Teach them the Chicken Dance

537. Play dress-up

538. Read with your children and have them read to you

539. Do not underestimate children's ability to understand the world around them. Discuss politics, social justice, and the larger world

540. Take educational vacations

541. Take eco-vacations

542. Take charity vacations

543. Remember, children always know what is going on in the house—don't hide family issues from them

544. Expect honesty from yourself and from your child

545. Teach restraint

546. Work with children on planning and decision-making skills

547. Promote self-esteem and personal power

548. Allow children to create a sense of purpose—a positive view of their personal future

549. Teach children the skills to just say no

550. Send them a postcard or greeting card in the mail and tell them something funny

551. If you have a teenager learning to drive, let them drive on the next errand and keep your mouth shut

552. Let your children pick out their favorite toy for Christmas to give to charity

553. Bring them to the dollar store and give them twenty dollars to buy anything for their friends

554. Let your child pick the dinner menu and help you prepare it

555. Go play in the puddles with your child—it's fun

556. Sit up close with your child and watch their favorite tv show

557. Play with your kids—create quality time

558. Dance with your children, and teach them to dance or sing or play a musical instrument

559. Listen to your child or your child's friends—do not judge, you may not even have to speak

560. Remember special occasions

561. Don't put work first. If work calls, make sure children understand that you work to provide a good home and a future for them

562. Practice and teach peaceful conflict resolution

563. Remember discipline is not punishment. Enforcing limits is teaching your child about how to live in a community

564. Swallow criticism, voice praise

565. Drop a handful of change near where the neighborhood kids play. It will brighten their day

566. Teach your child about God

567. Teach children to respect all humankind, including the homeless, the poor, the disabled, the abused, and the abandoned

568. Remember what makes your own heart sing

569. Praise the process as well as the product

570. Help children experience the delight of giving

571. Make personal time to laugh and play with each child

572. Make breakfast each morning

573. Make sure children's schedules are in line with time to rest and time to play

574. Teach good nutrition

575. Make sure children play physical games

576. Be a scout master

577. Participate in your athletic programs

578. Plant a fruit tree in your child's name and have the child contribute the harvest to a food pantry

579. Volunteer for community programs together—food pantries, clean-up programs

580. Have your children help organize a neighborhood event

581. Teach children to not personalize rejection

582. Be there for your child in good times and bad

583. Set socially acceptable behavior limits

584. Encourage individuality

585. Show your children every day that they are unconditionally loved

586. Practice joyful faith

587. Take your children to church

588. Be involved with church activities

589. Have game night at home—invite your children's friends

590. Limit media exposure—know what your children watch on tv and what sites they visit on the internet

591. Teach personal safety

592. Teach your teenager to drive

593. Punish disrespect to family members, neighbors, teachers, and elders

594. Take advantage of teachable moments

595. Let your child know expectations in terms of behavior and responsibilities. Be firm

596. Allow freedom of choice based on age and emotional maturity

597. Stay calm

598. Create a relationship with the parents of your children's friends

599. Confide in your children about appropriate issues they're old enough to understand

600. Teach your children about money—how to make it, how to use it, how to invest, and how to save

601. Don't limit children's ambitions

602. Teach cultural tolerance and the joys of diversity

603. Enforce bedtimes and curfews

604. Establish educational funds at birth

605. Make recycling a habit

606. Teach children about the environment

607. Make charity a habit

608. Plant a family garden and assign garden duties

609. Teach kids to cook

610. Make wildlife and nature education an adventure

611. Take a walk with your child

612. Encourage children to explore their art

613. Take a craft class together

614. Let your child teach you something new

615. Do not restrict food, but praise healthy choices

616. Never nag

617. Make sure to sees a pediatrician for regular check-ups and when problems arise

618. Let your children decide when to donate clothes, toys and sporting equipment to a worthy cause

619. Let your child earn rewards in real life

620. Encourage decision making—let older children pick out their own clothes

621. Realize that all kids will follow fads. Don't be judgmental

622. Teach kids to budget time and money

623. Know your own limits

624. Never hit your child

625. Intimidation is not discipline

626. Remember you are raising tomorrow's decision-makers

627. Work with your child to overcome failures and disappointments

628. Listen to your child's emotional needs and reflect back to them your understanding

629. Share your feelings with your child

630. Practice humility

631. Allow children time to work through issues. Give support when needed and back-off when needed

632. Don't take out your frustrations or lack of self-worth on your child

633. Emphasize the importance of family

634. Reevaluate what is "normal" on a regular basis

635. Keep pace with technology

636. Teach your children to pray, and pray with them daily

637. Do not smoke around your children

638. Practice good health habits—your children need you

639. Allow grandparents to have an active role in raising your children

640. Encourage the children's grandparents to have their own relationship with the children

641. Kids need to succeed

642. Don't try to fix everything for your children. Let them find solutions on their own

643. Take your kid for a day at your job. It will show them what you do each day and give them appreciation of what it takes to have a job

644. Open a savings account with your child. Teach her how money works

645. Make small investments with your children. Let them have a say in where the money goes and help them track its progress

646. Ask you children three "you" questions each day

Teens Helping Others

647. Sponsor a high school program on the importance of volunteering

648. On career day, ask the high school to set up a table where local nonprofits can solicit teen volunteers

649. Organize a teens-only food drive at school or church

650. Volunteer to babysit at a battered-women's shelter

651. Learn to knit and join *Guideposts* magazine's sweater project

652. Volunteer at your local Ronald McDonald House—cleaning, cooking, fundraising, babysitting, etc.

653. Become a sports coach for Special Olympics

654. Staff a Special Olympics event

655. Volunteer to be a walkathon participant and staffer

656. Help construct and maintain trails in a local state park

657. Become a nature guide

658. Become a local hospital volunteer

659. Start a study group with your friends in school—you will all learn together

660. Organize work crews through your school that would do work for people to raise money for a school project such as senior trip

661. Read to kids at your local library

662. Start an Internet training class at your local senior citizens center

663. Become a dog walker at the local animal shelter

664. Start a coat drive for the Salvation Army at your school

665. Plant trees on Arbor Day

666. Pick a candidate running for office whose ideas you believe in and volunteer to work for their campaign

667. Learn first aid

668. Become a life guard at the local pool

669. Become a summer-camp counselor

670. Join a sandbag crew when there is local flooding

671. Volunteer to create and/or maintain a website for a charity

672. Raise a puppy to become a service dog

673. Be a playground monitor at the local park playground

674. Volunteer at the local children's museum

675. Start a writing campaign with your friends to troops overseas

676. Collect Toys for Tots

677. Become an expert on a subject and give talks at local nursing homes, schools, and other programs

678. Mentor a younger person with problems

679. Join an environmental group and lead Save the Planet activities for Earth Day

680. Be an usher at your church

681. Volunteer for daycare at your church

682. Teach swimming classes

683. Volunteer for an area beautification program

684. Participate in community theater

685. Help organize a parade

686. Get your friends together and adopt a highway for clean-up

687. Go shopping for someone else

688. Form a Welcome to our School committee for new students—show them around the area, introduce them to new people, help them learn their new community

689. Start a charity car wash

690. Sell chocolates for the school band even if you are not part of the band

691. Learn all about the history of your area and give historical tours

692. Volunteer for a local haunted house for Halloween

693. Make back-to-school packages for less-advantaged kids

694. Teach someone to ice skate or roller skate

695. Volunteer to teach crafts at the library or community center

696. Become an assistant scout leader

697. Start a Pennies for Tomorrow program at your school—just collect pennies for a local good cause

698. Organize an awareness event to fund medical or crisis intervention in your community

699. Bake cookies for firefighters and police officers working on holidays

700. Start a babysitting service for firefighters and police officers so they can have date night with their spouses

701. Become a regular volunteer at your city hall

702. Put flags on veterans' graves in your local area for Memorial Day, Independence Day, and Veterans Day

703. Join a cemetery clean-up crew

704. Teach bike safety to young children as part of Bike Safety Week

705. Be a pooper scooper for the dog park

706. Join your church choir

707. Trick or treat for UNICEF

708. Hand out leaflets for an upcoming community event

709. Educate yourself on a local issue, such as homeless-ness, and become a community advocate

710. Donate blood

711. Join the local talent show

712. Look around the community and ask yourself—what can I do in the next hour to help?

713. Mentor your friends to become community volunteers

714. Help your friends—if you see a serious problem, help them out or intervene with their parents or authorities to get them help

715. Be a safe driver

716. Write down your goals and review them regularly

717. Write a community-news column for the local free paper

718. Volunteer for your local PBS pledge drive or auction—staff the phones, pick up items, etc.

719. Help seniors write letters and send holiday cards for Christmas

720. Lead your peers by example

721. Make I Care Kits with combs, toothbrushes, shampoo, etc., for the homeless

722. Adopt a senior citizen "grandfriend" and write him or her letters and call or visit regularly

723. Help a senior set up a Facebook page or open a Twitter account

724. Pick up groceries or medicine for someone in need

725. Deliver meals to homebound individuals

726. Hold an afternoon dance for your local nursing home

727. Paint a mural over graffiti

728. Plant flowers in public areas

729. Set up a buddy system for kids with special needs

730. Raise money to buy Braille books for the visually impaired

731. Bring toys to children in cancer wards

732. Adopt an acre of a rainforest

733. Create a habitat for wildlife

734. Learn to be a peer counselor

735. Give up your seat on the bus or train to someone else

736. Volunteer for a hotline

737. Hold a teddy bear drive for foster children, fire victims, etc.

738. Go caroling

739. Coordinate a book drive

740. Visit www.servenet.org to find volunteer opportunities in your area

Teach Kids About Money

741. As soon as they can count, introduce your children to money

742. Communicate with children about your values concerning money

743. Help children learn the difference between needs and wants

744. Set financial goals to teach the value of money and saving

745. Teach the value of saving versus spending

746. Give kids and allowance for chores

747. Take children to a credit union or bank to open their own savings account

748. Teach good record-keeping skills

749. Use shopping opportunities to teach budgeting

750. Allow kids to make spending decisions

751. Show children how to evaluate advertising

752. Alert kids to the dangers of borrowing

753. When you use a credit card, teach your kids how credit works

754. Establish a regular schedule for family discussions about finances

755. Take your child to an investment counselor

756. Start an investment portfolio with your child

757. Play Monopoly

758. Play the investment game, following stocks with play money for one year

759. Reward good choices

760. Introduce US Savings Bonds to kids

761. Encourage kids to start their own business—lawn mowing, babysitting, selling lemonade

762. Be an example of a good financial steward

763. Encourage teenagers to get a part-time job

764. Enroll them in Junior Achievement

765. Use every financial transaction as an opportunity to start a conversation about money

766. Share personal money experiences

767. Let kids start saving for their own college fund

Saving Children Everywhere

768. Adopt a child in need. Older children are the hardest to place

769. Become a foster parent, Big Brother, or Big Sister

770. Donate to and volunteer for your favorite child/family-oriented nonprofit organization

771. Become a camp counselor, teach at a Vacation Bible School, or pay a needy child's way to summer camp

772. Buy a Vacation Bible School kit for your parish

773. Become a volunteer tutor

774. Start a scholarship fund. It doesn't have to be a great deal of money

775. Sponsor a child's education—find a child in need and commit to providing clothes, food, educational materials, and possibly tuition

776. Donate to an international outreach food and health aid for children organization

777. Volunteer for a kids' sports group

778. Get sponsorships from local businesses to help offset your child's team's expenses

779. Donate sports equipment and school supplies to less-fortunate school districts

780. Read to kids

781. Buy clothes and toiletries for children without homes

782. Donate gently used clothing and supplies to clothing drives and thrift stores

783. Teach racial and cultural tolerance

784. Make lunches for needy kids

785. Encourage creativity and individuality in all children

786. If you suspect child abuse or neglect—report it

787. Respect parenting differences, especially with your children's friends

788. Remember birthdays of kids in your church and community

789. Shop at companies that support UNICEF

790. Educate yourself on programs in your community that work with disadvantaged children

791. Start internship programs in your company for disadvantaged teens

792. Rent out that basement apartment to a single mother for $1 a month

793. Work with the Salvation Army to hire disadvantaged parents at a decent salary

794. Do not do business with companies that use child, slave, or prison labor

795. Donate fans in the summer to disadvantaged families

796. Donate coats and blankets to disadvantaged families in the winter

797. Volunteer to teach job skills at the local homeless or women's shelter

798. Agree to babysit kids while parents attend job-skills classes

799. Volunteer to house foreign children and their families after medical treatment in the US

800. Organize a neighborhood yard sale with proceeds going to Save the Children

801. Volunteer for a mission vaccinating children in a third-world country

802. Volunteer to teach in a third-world country

803. Support Doctors Without Borders (www.doctorswithoutborders.org)

804. Join Habitat for Humanity

805. Support education programs for disadvantaged teens

806. Raise awareness of disadvantaged children in your own community—write articles, volunteer time, contribute funds and goods, speak out at public hearings

807. Sponsor a disadvantaged child at community center or through the scouts

808. Become a Big Brother/Big Sister

809. Adopt a family for back-to-school supplies

810. Purchase a computer and pay for Internet connection for a year for a disadvantaged family

811. Open a free daycare center for single mothers

812. Volunteer to read for the blind

813. Learn sign language (and teach your children)

814. Take a volunteering vacation to aid community projects in disadvantaged areas around the world

815. Pray for the children

816. Donate to international religious education

817. Support adult-education programs

818. Lobby local, state, and federal government on the rights of children

819. Encourage all children to succeed

Help Abused Kids

820. Report child abuse using the Childhelp USA National Child Abuse Hotline (www.childhelpusa.org)

821. Volunteer on a child-abuse hotline

822. Volunteer to work in a shelter for abused kids

823. Become a court-appointed advocate for children (www.casaforchildren.org)

824. Write a letter to your congressional representative expressing your concern about the foster care system and suggest reform

825. Start a child abuse prevention program in your community

826. Support a child abuse organization

827. Keep an eye out for kids in your neighborhood

828. Become a mentor

829. When a child reports abuse, believe him

830. Assure an abused child that it isn't her fault

831. Become an emergency foster parent

Kids Helping Kids

832. Arrange with your teacher to plant a school garden that everyone can enjoy

833. Ask a local business to donate a bench to put in the garden

834. Make a birdhouse for the garden

835. Pick up a pencil, crayon, books, etc. that your classmate dropped

836. Let the thirsty kid behind you get a drink at the drinking fountain first

837. Say hi to the new kid and play with him at recess

838. Let the kid who isn't athletic play on your team at recess

839. Tell a kid if she has toilet paper on her shoe

840. Compliment a classmates when they do a good job on something

841. Don't brag about your good grades to a kid who just got a bad grade on a paper

842. Help a friend who isn't getting good grades with his homework

843. Hold the door open for a kid or teacher who is carrying a lot of stuff

844. Pick up trash at recess and throw it away

845. Invite a new kid or shy kid to eat lunch with you

846. Clean up your mess at lunch and don't make a bigger mess by throwing food, spitting milk, throwing napkins on the ground, etc.

847. Don't stick gum under the desks or chairs

848. Help a new kid or younger kid find a classroom

849. If you see someone being bullied, tell an adult. If that adult doesn't do something, tell another. Keep telling until it stops

850. If they a friend is doing stuff that is dangerous, tell an adult

851. If a friend forgets his lunch or snack money, buy his lunch or share what you have

852. Let other kids suggest activities to play at recess—don't always be the one who says what everyone has to play

853. Start a Mission Club at school and collect money to donate to St. Vincent de Paul Society Catholic Charities, etc.

854. Tell someone if she has food in their teeth

855. Tell someone if his pants are unzipped

856. Help a kid find their ride home

857. Thank the teacher for helping you

858. Create an End Hunger Now club at your school

859. Start a Back to School drive to buy school supplies for kids in shelters

Helping Kids in Special Situations

860. Brighten up hospital rooms by creating decorations— paper flowers, leaves, snowflakes, raindrops, etc.

861. Many kids are bored in the hospital—give them paper, crayons, and colored markers to create their own art

862. Sick kids need a little cheer in their lives—get them books of jokes and volunteer to read funny materials

863. Distribute phone cards to kids in the hospital so they can call friends and loved ones

864. Become a pen pal to a child with a chronic illness

865. Throw a party for no reason with a few special friends for a child with a long-term illness

866. Learn all you can about the illness or special needs the child has

867. Ask lots of questions and listen to the answers given by doctors, insurance companies, schools, etc.

868. Always avoid the blame game

869. Learn American Sign Language

870. Support the Seeing Eye Dog Foundation (www.seeing eye.org)

871. Be a problem-solver, not a problem-maker—the child will benefit in the end

872. Become a futurist—think education, care, long-term prognosis, etc.

873. Really get to know child care providers and teachers and let them know you are there for them in support of the child

Advice Young Adults Don't Want to Hear

874. Show up for work

875. Show up for work on time

876. Deal with your debt before it gets worse

877. If you don't have credit, get some, but don't buy anything you can't afford

878. Don't screw over landlords or utility companies

879. Spend less than you earn

880. Drive safely, avoid accidents and tickets—it will cost you later

881. Don't rush to buy all the expensive toys and trappings of adult life

882. Start saving and investing for retirement now

883. Learn about money—how to earn it, how to save it, how to invest it

884. Start an emergency fund

885. Get health insurance

886. Exercise regularly

887. Eat right

888. Don't eat out all the time—learn to cook for yourself

889. Get enough sleep

890. Keep your resumé up-to-date

891. Network, network, network

892. Put time and energy into friendships

893. Thank those who inspired you along the way

894. Find a mentor

895. Watch out for on-the-job romances

896. Keep learning

897. Establish long- and short-term goals

898. Enjoy life and all the things that come with youth

899. Be patient

900. Don't expect instant gratitude

901. Don't take shortcuts

902. Understand that your morals are an important part of you

903. Learn from your mistakes

904. Make a list of 100 things you want to do in the next five years—some practical, some not so practical

905. Understand that the tax man always cometh

Your Spouse Is Your Best Friend—Show It!

906. Finish putting away the laundry your spouse hasn't finished

907. Unexpectedly do a chore no one really likes to do—clean a bathroom or the fish tank so your spouse doesn't have to do it

908. Secretly fill the gas tank of your spouse's vehicle

909. Clean out and wash your spouse's car

910. Help your children make an unexpected gift for your spouse

911. Help your children make a cake or something your spouse likes to eat

912. Smile every time you see your spouse

913. Ask her how she is while looking in their eyes

914. Give your spouse a big hug for no reason

915. Make a coupon book of fun things you can do with your spouse

916. Hold hands

917. Play hide-and-seek with your spouse

918. Take an interest in your spouse's work

919. Send your spouse a text message with good news

920. Run a hot bath, light a candle, and sit and chat together

921. Wake your partner with a kiss and a hug

922. Buy tickets and attend a game/event with an open mind—even if you're not a fan

923. While your spouse is in the shower, put a fresh bath towel in the dryer and so he has a nice warm towel when they get out

924. Make her favorite dessert "just because"

925. Give back rubs and foot massages without being asked

926. Leave a song on his voicemail that reminds you of him, a song that has meaning to both of you

927. Send a valentine to your spouse on a dreary November day

928. Plant a ten-second do-it-like-you-mean-it kiss on her when she least expects it

929. Put a love note in her lunch

930. Say "I Love You" on a regular basis

931. Put a love note under his pillow

932. Put a love note on the bathroom mirror

933. Surprise her by making her favorite meal—then do the dishes together afterward

934. Give your spouse remote control

935. Go to the library and check out some books your spouse has been wanting to read

936. Listen, listen, listen—and then listen some more!

937. Offer to run carpools for the children when you can—it doesn't matter who has driven more

938. Plan a fun activity you and your children so your spouse can have some free time

939. Don't forget anniversaries, birthdays, etc. You don't have to spend money—make something or do something for him instead

940. Tell her you love her as many times a day as you can!

941. Watch a movie or do an activity you know your spouse would love

942. Listen when your spouse says he needs something—and surprise him by getting it for him!

943. Listen when your spouse says something is broken, a light bulb is out, etc.—and fix it for her!

944. Put a song your spouse has said she loves on her iPod without her knowing—it will be such a surprise to see it there!

945. Arrange a conference call with your in-laws so your spouse can talk to everyone at once and catch up on what is going on with everyone in the family

946. Help your spouse be healthy—exercise with him, remind her to make her yearly check-up appointments, take vitamins together, prepare healthy meals together

947. Support your spouse's weight-loss program and efforts to incorporate a healthy lifestyle into your marriage

948. Write your spouse a poem

949. Renew your vows

New Child Born

950. When buying new-baby gifts, concentrate on items and services needed over the next year, not just the next few weeks

951. Consider cloth diapers—better for the environment

952. Give a year of diaper service

953. Buy a year of formula

954. Give new parents a Netflix subscription—they will be home lots of nights

955. Provide a baby-safe house kit with electric outlet covers and cabinet locks

956. Call ahead and offer to make a full meal for the family with the newborn

957. Give new parents a baby monitor

958. Gift new parents child-safety seats

959. Collect coupons for diapers, baby wipes, formula, baby food, baby cereal, etc., for new moms

960. Help mom and dad set up and paint the nursery

961. Make a baby quilt

962. Wash baby's bedding before giving to remove all the chemicals

963. Give a gift card for a fast-food restaurant to the family

964. Invite the husband and other children to come to your house for supper and playtime so Mom and the new baby can have some time alone

965. Invite Mom to come to your house for supper alone so she can have some time away

966. Make a "wreath" of diapers, rattles, onesies, etc., for the expectant mother

967. Offer to do laundry for the family

968. If they are using disposable diapers, save coupons from the newspaper for them and give them to the family

969. Offer to do the grocery shopping for the family while you are doing your own shopping

970. Offer to run errands, go to the post office, drop off dry cleaning, etc., while you're out doing your own errands

971. Plant a fruit tree in celebration of the child's birth

972. Each year as the fruit ripens, harvest the fruit for a food bank

973. As the child grows, have her help you harvest the fruit and take it to the food pantry

974. Volunteer to babysit while Mom takes a nap or a shower, writes thank you notes, makes phone calls, pays bills, watches her favorite tv show, updates the baby book, etc.

975. Quilt (or join a quilt group) small, soft covers for premies

976. Listen to the new mom—don't constantly give her advice or tell her what she is doing wrong

977. Offer to pick up restaurant takeout for the family

978. Give the new mom contact information for parenting groups and organizations in the area she may be interested in joining

979. If you've used a good daycare or preschool, let her know about them

980. Organize a get-together for the new mom and baby when the baby is at least 3 months old. Mom can show off the baby, who is now having her shots and can be around other babies safely

Anonymous (and Not-So-Anonymous) Good Deeds for Adults

981. Buy dessert for the table next to yours

982. Cut someone's grass

983. Weed someone's garden

984. Wash someone's car

985. Pay for food ordered by the car behind you at a drive-thru window

986. Pay for the movie for the third person in line behind you

987. Give a fifty-dollar tip to a bag boy at the grocery store

988. Make arrangements to pay for utility bills for someone in need

989. Buy someone else's gas while they are filling up

990. Drop off a bag of groceries on someone's doorstep

991. Pay for a neutering of a senior's pet

992. Pick up every garbage can on the street on a windy day

993. Take ice cream and cookies to a local nursing home

994. Decorate for Christmas a small, isolated, miserable looking tree near an area frequented by lots of people

995. Send a catered meal to a senior citizens center

996. Anonymously donate $1 million to a school of your choice for scholarships

997. Bring coffee to everyone waiting for a bus on a Monday morning

998. Give a waitress a gift certificate for an all-day spa treatment

999. Organize a fashion show at a Weight Watchers meeting

1000. Buy fifty turkeys and have a school give them out to parents in need for the holidays

1001. Give your winning lottery ticket to a charity

1002. Set up a shoe-shine stand and don't charge anyone

1003. Buy several hamburgers and pass them out to homeless people

1004. Buy a dozen long-stemmed roses and pass them out to every woman on the street

1005. Wait until someone is hailing a cab, and while they're getting in pay the fare

1006. Hand a horse-mounted police officer a gift certificate for lunch and an apple for his/her horse

1007. Hand out bus or subway tokens at the stop

1008. Tip the bus driver ten dollars

1009. On a hot day, hand out ice-cold drinks to road workers

1010. On a cold day, hand out hot drinks to road workers

Great Questions to Ask Family and Friends

1011. What was the happiest moment of your life?

1012. What was the saddest moment of your life?

1013. What is your first memory of me?

1014. Tell me about the most important person in your life

1015. Who has been the biggest influence on your life?

1016. What lessons influenced you?

1017. Where will you be in ten years?

1018. Who has been the kindest to you in your life?

1019. What are the most important lessons you've learned in life?

1020. What is your earliest memory?

1021. Are there any words of wisdom you'd like to pass along to me?

1022. What makes us like each other?

1023. Is there anything you've always wanted to tell me?

1024. What are you proudest of in your life?

1025. When in life have you felt most alone?

1026. How has your life been different than what you'd imagined?

1027. How would you describe yourself?

1028. How would you like to be remembered?

1029. Do you have any regrets?

1030. What does your future hold?

1031. Is there anything you've never told me but want to tell me now?

1032. Is there something about me you've always wanted to know but have never asked?

1033. Do you remember any songs you used to sing?

1034. How has society changed you?

1035. How did your job change you?

1036. How did you know you were in love?

1037. How did you pick path you're on?

Give a Part of Yourself

1038. Donate blood

1039. Donate platelets

1040. Donate your hair to Locks of Love to make wigs for cancer patients

1041. Donate old prescription eyeglasses to the Lions Club

1042. Donate your body to science or a medical school

1043. Make an apheresis blood donation

1044. Become an organ donor

1045. Donate your car to the Salvation Army instead of selling it for a couple of hundred bucks—and you'll get a tax write-off!

1046. Volunteering to drive seniors or the very sick to the doctor

1047. Join (or start) your church's committee that prepares meals for people who've had a death in the family and for mourners after the funeral

1048. Donate your used books and magazines to health care centers, donation centers, neighbors, etc.

1049. Take your used magazines to a hospital emergency room or waiting room and leave them on the table

1050. Use your skills to teach others

1051. Volunteer to spread the word about organ donation or to have an event to raise awareness

1052. Join the blood/bone marrow national donation registry, and be prepared to donate if you are a match

1053. Donate cord blood after you have a baby

1054. If a spouse or relative needs a kidney transplant, consider being tested and being the donor

1055. During natural disasters, open your house to the victims

1056. If the local highway closes in a snow storm, work with your parish to open its doors to the stranded—organize hot coffee, food, and baby supplies

Save the Planet

1057. Help conserve energy and keep the air quality high by taking public transportation when possible—or walking or riding your bike

1058. Combine trips whenever possible

1059. Don't litter

1060. Plant a shade tree outside your home can save energy and give our feathered friends a home

1061. Save water by taking shorter showers and installing a low-flow showerhead

1062. Buy products with less packaging or buy in bulk

1063. Choose paper or cardboard over plastics

1064. Save paper—print on both sides

1065. Replace chemical cleaners with nontoxic products

1066. Take yourself off mailing lists for products in which you have no interest

1067. Carpool

1068. Don't run the washing machine until you have a full load

1069. Volunteer at a river clean-up

1070. Donate to endangered-species projects such as Save the Manatee Club

1071. Get regular tune-ups and oil changes

1072. Make your next new car a hybrid or high-mileage vehicle

1073. Use energy-saving light bulbs

1074. Turn your thermostat down three degrees in the winter and up three degrees in the summer

1075. Start a compost bin

1076. Buy reusable products—one cloth coffee filter can replace 300 paper filters

1077. Invest in socially responsible mutual funds and companies

1078. Reinstall a clothesline—remember the wonderful smell of sun-dried sheets and towels?

1079. Buy paint that does not contain VOCs (volatile organic chemicals)

1080. Turn off the water while brushing your teeth—you could save 1800 gallons of clean water a year

1081. Don't be a "butt-tosser"—dispose of cigarette butts property

1082. Purchase rechargeable batteries

1083. Recycle old batteries

1084. Avoid pesticides and herbicides in your house, lawn, and garden

1085. Fight mosquitoes by putting up bat houses—bats love mosquito dinners

1086. Organize a Clean up the Parish committee

1087. Set a good example for your children and others by always throwing your trash away

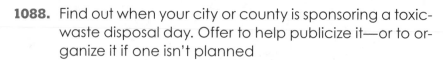

1088. Find out when your city or county is sponsoring a toxic-waste disposal day. Offer to help publicize it—or to organize it if one isn't planned

1089. Organize a clean-up day for the local scout troop

1090. Participate in recycle programs—paper, cans, plastics, etc.

1091. Watch the weather—on the bad air-quality days, don't drive more than you need to, don't mow the lawn, etc.

1092. Plant trees, shrubs, a garden—all green plants help keep the air clean

1093. Donate to an organization that provides bees to indigent farmers to provide them with honey to eat and sell and bees to pollinate their crops

1094. Try to not use fertilizer, weed killers, etc.

1095. Many of the things we use don't break down in landfills—plastics, electrical appliances and components—etc. Use them sparingly and dispose of them properly when they're no longer used

1096. Dispose of old computer monitors and TVs carefully—many computer stores recycle them for free

1097. Don't water the lawn and wash the car when there is a drought

1098. Think of ways to conserve water with your family and make it a priority

1099. Organize a committee in the neighborhood to plant shrubs, flowers, etc. in the common areas

1100. Create a community compost heap and spread the word that anyone can contribute to it and anyone can use it

1101. Create your own compost heap and use it instead of chemicals

1102. Participate in a highway clean-up program

1103. Organize a group to pick up trash in a local park

1104. Help fix broken equipment at a local park

1105. Organize a kids' field trip to a local nursery. Ask a staff member to talk about plants that grow well in your area, planting season, care needed, etc.

1106. Organize a garden club in your neighborhood and meet once a month or so and share the bounty—whether vegetables, fruit, flowers, etc.

1107. Help organize an Earth Day committee at your child's school, at your work, your scout troop, etc. Teach participants about the history of Earth Day and what they can do to help keep the planet green and healthy

1108. Take your family on a walk in the woods—look at the flora and fauna and enjoy

1109. Help your children learn about the rainforest

1110. Give a presentation on the rainforest to your child's class

1111. See if your office is using eco-friendly office products. Your company may be able to join with other companies to purchase in bulk and thus bring the prices down

1112. Use recycled bags instead of plastic bags from the grocery stores

1113. Set up a rain barrel at your house and use the water later for your plants and garden

1114. Turn off lights you're not using

1115. Don't turn on the TV unless you're watching it

1116. If you can afford it, volunteer to travel to help somewhere in the country that has experienced an oil spill, a natural disaster, etc.

1117. Implement energy-saving measures in your home, such as solar panels, energy-saving washer and dryer, energy-saving water heater, etc.

1118. Use recycled paper products

1119. Think twice before buying disposable products

1120. Clean and replace air filters when recommended

1121. Recycle plastic shopping bags

1122. Use the stairs instead of the elevator

1123. Store food in reusable containers instead of plastic wrap or aluminum foil

1124. Learn about conservation issues in your area

1125. Teach children to respect the land

1126. Promote land-stewardship programs

1127. Education yourself on the proposed carbon tax

1128. Talk to management at your job about implementing other conservation practices such as recycling printer cartridges, solar power, recycling trash, composting, etc.

1129. Ask if you can start a company garden and get everyone involved in growing—and eating—the fruits of their labor!

1130. See if your company and coworkers will sponsor a student group to learn more about conservation

1131. Conserve energy by hanging your clothes out to dry instead of using the dryer (some subdivisions and communities have rules against this, so check before doing this)

1132. Conserve energy by walking or riding your bike when possible

1133. Switch your gas-powered lawn mower for an old-fashioned push-mower with no engine

1134. Search environmental websites for information on how to make your house more energy efficient

1135. Turning down your water heater to 120 degrees saves energy and is much safer if you have small children or elderly living in your household

1136. Ask your utility company if it makes free home-energy evaluations

1137. When purchasing new appliances, look for those approved by the EPA or other reputable organization to be energy efficient

1138. Ask if you can work from home some days to save on gasoline consumption and emissions

1139. Donate to a nonprofit that is researching alternative energy sources—wind power, solar power, etc.

1140. Consider cremation

1141. Consider natural burial

1142. Ask your pharmacy how to safely dispose of expired or unused medications (don't flush down the toilet)

10 Ways to Save 10 Gallons of Water

1143. Install a low-flow showerhead for each bathroom

1144. Turn water off when brushing teeth

1145. Use "old" water from pet bowls to water plants

1146. Don't rinse dishes before putting in dishwasher

1147. Use run-off water from washing vegetables to water plants

1148. Don't wash your car at home

1149. Don't powerwash sidewalks, driveways, or decks

1150. Take a shower instead of a bath

1151. Install a graywater system

1152. Permaculture as much as possible

Stop Global Warming

1153. Clean or replace filters on your furnace and air conditioner every three months

1154. Do not leave appliances on standby

1155. Replace regular incandescent light bulbs with compact fluorescent bulbs

1156. Buy only energy-efficient appliances

1157. Carefully consider which electronics you really need and use (including appliances) and which ones you just want

1158. Cover your pots when cooking

1159. Move your fridge and freezer away from the stove to save energy

1160. Defrost old fridges and freezers regularly

1161. Install a programmable thermostat

1162. Replace your old single-glazed windows with double-glazing

1163. Wrap your water heater in an insulation blanket

1164. Don't let heat escape from your house over a long period

1165. Get a home energy audit

1166. Use a clothesline instead of a dryer whenever possible

1167. Recycle your organic waste

1168. Buy locally grown and produced foods

1169. Buy fresh foods instead of frozen

1170. Seek out and support local farmers' markets

1171. Buy organic food as much as possible

1172. Buy only free-trade international products

1173. Eat less meat

1174. Don't leave an empty roof rack on your car—the weight uses more gas

1175. Buy clothes made of organic fabrics

1176. Try telecommuting from home

1177. Fly less

1178. Encourage your school, business, and community buildings to reduce emissions

1179. Join the virtual march

1180. Encourage the switch to renewable energy

1181. Protect and conserve forest worldwide

1182. If remodeling, consider installing solar power or other alternative energy sources

1183. If building, use only "green" construction

Support Alternative Transportation

1184. If your community has mass transit, use it

1185. If your community has no mass transit, contact your legislators and corporate leaders about plans for such a system

1186. Volunteer time and skill to maintain or help bring about mass transit

1187. Use your feet instead of the motorized wheel

1188. Carpool whenever possible

1189. Pedal whenever possible

1190. Make the new car electric or a hybrid

1191. Educate yourself on the new technologies that are appearing at a blinding pace

1192. Vote for politicians working for mass transit and/or alternatives to the single-driver gas-driven vehicle

1193. Buy a car that gets good gas mileage

1194. Combine your errands into one trip

1195. If you're a merchant, offer discounts or special services or products for those who walk, bike, skate, or take the subway to your place of business

1196. If you're an employer, offer incentives for your employees to carpool or take mass transit or walk

1197. Support community projects like bike lanes and walking lanes

Invest Green

1198. Read news stories about companies that help the environment

1199. Invest in a company that has a strong record of community relations and involvement

1200. Invest in companies that treat employees well

1201. Know a company's foreign policy before you invest

1202. Choose to shop locally when possible

1203. Avoid investing in companies with shady business practices

1204. Remove stocks from your portfolio that do not meet your "green" standards

1205. Research mutual funds and the companies involved

1206. Don't pick investment funds on return alone

1207. Be involved as a shareholder

1208. Check Merrill Lynch's new tool, Energy Efficiency Index (EEI), to identify companies and their environmental impact

1209. Invest in companies that produce products that are sustainable

1210. Invest in companies that are making wise financial and business choices

1211. Invest in companies that promote green workplaces

1212. Analyze where your 401(k) and IRA are invested

1213. Lend money through KIVA (www.kiva.org)

1214. Invest in companies that invest in people

Helping Farmers

1215. Attend an agriculture-related event

1216. Get kids involved in local 4-H programs

1217. Give to agriculture-related nonprofits

1218. Teach someone to garden

1219. Donate subscriptions to farm periodicals to your local library

1220. Buy local

1221. Learn about your family and community agricultural heritage

1222. Support the Land Institute (www.landinstitute.org)

1223. Network for farmers

1224. Promote good land stewardship

1225. Learn about bioenergy

1226. Support bumble-bee preservation and conservation

1227. Buy fewer processed foods

1228. Support agricultural education

1229. Work with disaster and emergency-relief services

1230. Provide legal advice

1231. Provide financial and credit-counseling service

1232. Learn what the Farm Bill is all about

1233. Support better farming research

1234. Support Future Farmers of America

1235. Join a farm group

1236. Write an editorial on the importance of farming

1237. Support human rights

1238. Volunteer for Farm Aid (www.farmaid.org)

1239. Buy at farmers' markets

1240. Promote farm-fresh foods in school cafeterias

1241. Purchase only meat and animal products from humanly raised sources

1242. Know where your food comes from

1243. Support world food programs

1244. Support the Growing Good Food Movement

1245. Download and read Farm to School 101 at www. farmaid.org

1246. Tell Congress to support family farming

For the Troops & Veterans

1247. Find an organization that puts together care packages for our troops in foreign countries and donate items for the packages/donate money to help with the postage

1248. Adopt a military family who has a parent stationed overseas—in Iraq or Afghanistan—and help the parent who is at home with the children

1249. Volunteer to babysit, do chores, play with the children, take them to the park

1250. Donate a cell phone to a deployed soldier

1251. Give to the Marines' Toys for Tots

1252. Volunteer at a veterans facility

1253. Pray for all those in service

1254. Thank someone in the military

1255. If you see a member of the armed forces on a long flight, buy them lunch or a drink

1256. Send cards to recovering soldiers at Walter Reed Army Medical Center in Washington, DC

1257. Send several copies of Liguori's new *Reveille for the Soul: Prayers for Military Life* to the soldiers and veterans you know or to a military or veteran's hospital

1258. Donate frequent flyer miles to Operation Hero Miles (www.heromiles.org)

1259. Take a veteran out to eat

1260. Knit or crochet a scarf and donate it to a local VFW for a veteran in need

1261. Listen to veterans' stories with interest

1262. Support a military family through Operation Homefront's Adopt-a-Family Program

1263. Military member at the same restaurant as you? Send them a drink or pay for their dessert

1264. Is there a disabled veteran in your neighborhood? Help with the raking of his leaves or shoveling her driveway

1265. Make a web page dedicated to our military

1266. Make an apple pie or another dessert for a neighborhood veteran

1267. Hang a sign in your business window and invite all veterans in for something free—a cup of coffee, a flower, a massage—something you can give from your inventory to show your gratitude

1268. Make a quilt for a retiring service member. It will be a keepsake they treasure

1269. Host a special luncheon for all of your veterans on your staff—recognize their service to your company and your country

1270. Send a note to your local school to urge the teachers to discuss Veterans Day

1271. In November, celebrate Military Family Month

1272. Give a military family your phone number and ask them to call if they need help around the house

1273. Make a note to call them this winter to see what they need

1274. Have your children paint a picture or write a letter. Send it to a relative who is a veteran

1275. Recognize the veterans in church on the Sunday before or after Veterans Day

1276. Greet them on their special day with a smile and a thank you

1277. Remember veterans during other holidays, especially those who don't have families

1278. Teach your children a patriotic song, like "America the Beautiful" or the "Star-Spangled Banner"

1279. Give the veterans in your company a paid afternoon off on Veterans Day

1280. Offer a military discount year round and include veterans

1281. If you give a military discount, you'll get a free ad on militaryavenue.com. Invite a Veteran to a class or to the entire school

1282. Pray for them and their families every day

1283. Ask local businesses to participate in a drive for local veterans or deployed service members

1284. Clean out your closets and contribute gently used household goods to Vietnam Veterans of America

1285. Do a random and anonymous act of kindness for a vet or their family

1286. Use social networking—Facebook, Twitter—to thank vets for their service

1287. Open your house on Thanksgiving or another holiday to a few veterans (active-duty or prior-service) who don't have any family in the area. Visit Arlington National Cemetery, the Vietnam Veterans Wall, or any of the other War Memorials on your next trip to DC

1288. Call a veteran friend and get together over dinner or a movie

1289. Help a deployed single service member by taking care of their pet while they are gone; get involved with a Pet Foster Care program

1290. Invite a few vets and friends over on Veterans Day and celebrate their service over beer, a football game, movie or game of pool in the basement

1291. Talk to your children about the pride we have in the military

1292. Visit your local USO What do they need?

1293. Fly your flag every day of the year. Don't forget to lower it when appropriate

1294. Teachers: Have your kids write short articles of how veterans are honored around the world. And if you know any veterans locally, propose that your kids interview them about what it's like to serve in the US military

1295. Learn a fact about the particular branch of service your family member has joined

1296. Are you a military brat? Talk to your parents about the pride you have in their service

1297. Hear the National Anthem playing? Stop what you are doing and think about the sacrifices of our US military

1298. Wear an American flag on your clothing. It's a small way to say, "I am proud of my country"

1299. Introduce your children to VA Kids, from the Department of Veterans Affairs

1300. Have a pot-luck, at church or a banquet hall, for a group of local veterans Invite the community to participate

1301. Vote

1302. Request a patriotic song in a soldier's honor on the radio

1303. Tell your children all about your veteran grandparents

1304. Give military folks a big smile as you walk by

1305. If you see a veteran with an old flag, leave them a new one with a note of thanks for their service

1306. Find out which businesses in your community truly support veterans and the troops and become their customer

1307. Do you know the mom or dad of a veteran? Thank them for raising one of America's Heroes

1308. Go to your local VFW ask if you can make a donation, either by money or donation of your time. If you have a family member that serves in the armed forces you could make a donation in there honor

1309. In the market to hire? Seriously consider a veteran (http://hirevetsfirstdol.gov/). Meditate on these words: "O Lord God of hosts, stretch forth, we pray, your almighty arm to strengthen and protect the soldiers of our country. Support them in the day of battle, and in the time of rest and training keep them safe from all evil. Endue them with courage and loyalty; and grant that in all things they may serve without reproach; through Jesus Christ our Lord Amen."—From the *Book of Worship for United States Forces*

1310. Proudly display an "I support the troops" magnet on the bumper of your car

1311. Know a veteran that will be flying soon? Give them your upgrade coupon for their next flight

1312. During a family reunion recognize the veterans in your family A special toast or a big family "Thank you!"

1313. Organize a group (boys scouts, girl scouts, classroom) to write letters to veterans. Bring the letters & cards to a local nursing home to be delivered to their vets

1314. Support our troops this holiday season via Red Cross Holiday Mail for Heroes program

1315. Is it still warm where you live? Treat a veteran to a round of golf on Veterans Day or the weekend before or after

1316. Attend a local parade or ceremony on Veterans Day

1317. Make a tax-deductible donation to Books For Soldiers. They send books and other care packages to our deployed service members

1318. Help a veteran with projects around his or her house. Patching a leaky roof, moving heavy rocks or rearranging the living room furniture is easier for the twentysomethings than sixtysomethings

1319. Make a lunch date: Take your veteran colleague out for lunch

1320. Learn to say Thank You in sign language

1321. Ask your company to put a flag out. Offer to help with raising & lowering the flag

1322. Offer to take a veteran's dog for a walk Invite them to come along with you if they can

1323. Know a veteran's hobby? Send a subscription to a related magazine

1324. Offer to babysit for a military family. Let the husband and wife get out together on Veterans Day or over the weekend. Perhaps it will be a great opportunity for them to reconnect after a deployment

1325. Order a copy of *Prayers for Our Armed Forces* from Liguori for everyone you know with a loved one in the military

Friends With Posttraumatic Stress Disorder

1326. Learn everything you can about PTSD

1327. Exercise together

1328. Don't judge

1329. Be there to listen

1330. Show respect

1331. Look out for them and life's problem areas

1332. Allow room for mistakes

1333. Talk positively

1334. Give them there space

1335. Be active together

1336. Plan and participate in activities with friends and family

1337. Love them

1338. Don't belittle them or what they experience

1339. Be patient

1340. Understand that you have not experienced their world (unless you really have, then share those experiences in a positive way)

1341. Avoid harsh remarks

1342. Encourage their self-esteem

1343. Take care of yourself

1344. Take threats seriously

1345. Talk to them about self-destructive behaviors

1346. Seek out advice from professionals

Fun in the Sun

1347. Carry an extra trash bag with you the beach As you walk in and out of the beach area, pick up any trash you see—make sure to recycle the soda cans and plastic water bottles

1348. Join a bird rescue group Pelicans, gulls and cranes get caught in old fishing line and nets left by careless humans

1349. Pick up and dispose of old fishing line, hooks and netting as you come upon it

1350. Bring extra water to the beach—so many people forget to stay hydrated—share with those near by Also, consider bringing extra sunscreen and spray-on antibiotic

1351. Plan a trip to one of the many beaches that host sea turtles—pick a time when the eggs will be hatching

1352. Help clean up the Gulf of Mexico coast line after a hurricane

1353. Protest illegal dumping in oceans

1354. Join a sea bird rescue group

1355. Wear sunscreen

1356. Invite friends outside (5 minutes of sun a day)

1357. Play with children outside

1358. Organize a neighborhood picnic

1359. Support local juvenile sports

1360. Talk a walk

1361. Go camping

1362. Go fishing

1363. Learn to golf

1364. Sail around the world

1365. Hold a family jubilee in the park

1366. Feed the ducks at the local pond

1367. Visit the botanical garden near you

1368. Go to a springtime plant sale, and buy and plant

1369. Learn to water ski

1370. Take a bike ride

1371. Visit a Living History farm

1372. Organize a nature walk with the neighborhood kids

1373. Take up lawn bowling

1374. Join a chess game in the park

1375. Mow the lawn

1376. Volunteer to be playground monitor at school

1377. Adopt a highway, and join a road-cleaning crew

1378. Stand on a soap box and speak your peace

1379. Sell Girl Scout cookies in front of a grocery store

1380. Go to an outdoor church service

1381. If you are a teacher, take your lessons outside

1382. If you are a business person, take the next meeting outside

1383. Take up lunchtime walks with a coworker

1384. Learn to hula-hoop

1385. Become a lifeguard on the beach or at your local pool

1386. Walk your dog, and your neighbor's dog too

1387. Go to a baseball game

1388. Organize an afternoon tea

1389. Open a lemonade stand with your kids

1390. Organize a block party

1391. Organize a petition drive for your favorite cause and hit the sidewalks

1392. Stomp door to door for your favorite politician

1393. Volunteer for pet-adoption day in the park

1394. Attend a local craft fair

1395. Visit a Renaissance fair

1396. Attend the county fair

1397. Take a wine-country tour

1398. Join a group of farm workers for the day

1399. Volunteer for cemetery clean-up

1400. Hold a family reunion in the park

1401. Have a hayride

1402. Go on a cattle-trail drive

1403. Bike or run across country

1404. Join a parade

1405. Bird watch

1406. Volunteer for a seasonal bird count

1407. Ride in a hot-air balloon

1408. Go swimming with your kids or godchildren

Fun in the Snow

1409. Bundle up and make sure everyone is adequately clothed for the temperatures

1410. Learn to ski

1411. Learn to snowboard

1412. Build a snowman

1413. Have a snowball fight

1414. Organize a shoveling party and shovel all the public walkways in the neighborhood

1415. Learn to snowshoe

1416. Knock heavy snow off bushes and other plants

1417. Take a nature walk in the snow

1418. Cut down your own Christmas tree (where it's allowed)

1419. Clean off your neighbor's car

1420. Make a snow angel (no matter how old you are)

1421. Put down plant-safe ice melt in icy spots

1422. Ask an elderly or disabled neighbor if they need anything from the store before you head out

1423. Go tobogganing

1424. Take an avalanche-education class

1425. If you put down cardboard in the gutter to gain traction, remove it once you're out

1426. Set up a hot-chocolate stand (or hot cider)

1427. Collect maple syrup

1428. Have a marshmallow roast in your backyard

1429. Invite your neighbors on a snowbird watch

1430. Catch a snowflake on your tongue

1431. If it's sunny, wear sunscreen

1432. Have a living-room slumber party in front of the fire and tell ghost stories

1433. Call family members to make sure they are OK during and after the storm

1434. Be prepared for power failures with flashlights, blankets, candles, etc.

1435. Check on neighbors

1436. Take homeless to shelters

1437. Take homeless into your home

1438. Check on new moms to be sure they have all the supplies they need

1439. See someone on the street, take them for a meal and hot coffee

1440. Donate coats and blankets to the homeless and working poor

1441. Drive your kids to school, invite neighborhood kids along for the ride

1442. Drive safe

1443. Carry sand (or kitty litter) in your vehicle

1444. Enjoy God's diversity

Travel With Care

1445. Traveling on the bus, airplane, train, etc.—where there are many other people from different backgrounds—be careful what you say and do. Act and speak respectfully, don't make comments about other people, don't smoke or be loud, etc.

1446. Traveling with a group can be a lot of fun! It's nice to pack extra tissues, handwipes, etc., to share with your companions. If you pack a snack, pack something that can be shared

1447. Be a good traveling companion when traveling in a group and help out when someone is having trouble with their baggage, getting their tickets, not knowing where to go in an airport or train station, etc.

1448. It pays to be nice to the people working on the planes, trains, at the car rental place, etc. Smile and compliment them

1449. If you are traveling with a child, it is your responsibility to keep your child occupied and quiet. Take plenty of snacks, games, etc., and take advantage of this special uninterrupted time you have with your child

1450. If you see another parent traveling and their kids are in meltdown, lend a hand with luggage and the kids— one parent to another

1451. Remember, no one wants to hear your telephone conversation while sitting next to you on a plane, bus, train, etc. Put the phone down and read a book, or use text messaging

1452. If you are done with a magazine or newspaper while on a plane, offer it to your neighbor. Even if they don't want it, it's a nice gesture

1453. Don't drink too much alcohol while traveling. It is very disruptive, and you may find yourself in handcuffs and being escorted off the flight at the next stop!

1454. Offer to switch seats if you see a family is separated because they couldn't get seats together

1455. Offer to switch seats if you see someone has been put in the exit aisle but shouldn't have been

1456. Be respectful of other passengers and don't kick the back of their seats, lean back into the person behind you, hog the armrests, etc. Respect works both ways and people will treat you well if you treat them well

1457. When traveling in another country, learn the manners and customs before arriving

1458. Learn to say hello, goodbye, yes, no, thank you, and please in the language of the country you are visiting

1459. If giving gifts to your host is a custom in the port of call, bring gifts that are specific to your country and made in your country. They do not have to be expensive, but they do need to be memorable

1460. If traveling internationally on business, familiarize yourself with the business customs of that country. Bow, shake hands, embrace, kiss on the check, business cards with two hands, tip, not to tip?

1461. When leaving a foreign country, give all your leftover currency to charity or to someone in that country

1462. Do not assume that everyone speaks English

1463. Remember, as a tourist, you are a guest—act it

1464. Remember, you are an unofficial ambassador for your country—act it

1465. Sample local cuisine

1466. Frequent local businesses

1467. Do not brag about how great (or how much better) your own country is or how successful you are there

1468. Take an eco-tourism trip and leave a small footprint

1469. Take a humanitarian vacation. Volunteer to work on needed projects in poor areas

1470. If you're in the medical profession, consider using your skills in a third-world country

1471. If you are traveling to a poor country, ask your host if there is something you might bring that would help someone in need—extra toiletries, blankets, simple medical supplies

1472. Bring photos of your family and home. It is fun for your hosts to see where you come from

1473. Seek out cultural events and entertainment—it aids in your understanding of the place you are visiting

1474. Respect clothing customs—if women wear headcloths, bring one with you; if shorts are not allowed in the temple, bring a wraparound skirt

1475. Go paperless in making your travel arrangements—use the Internet

1476. Sign the "Responsible Traveler" pledge at www. globalproblems-globalsolutions.org/site/Page Navigator/FWH_survey_travelPledge

1477. Support sustainable tourism programs

1478. When traveling to poorer countries, book responsibly. If you are using chain hotels or tour operators, learn more about how they treat their employees

1479. Minimize your waste. Carry a reusable shopping bag Dispose of all trash according to local rules. That includes the use of toilets

1480. Lend a hand—make a positive impact on your host country. Pick up trash, offer to help seniors, etc. (the same manners you would have at home)

1481. Buy souvenirs from local artisans—it helps out their economy

1482. If nature touring, know which species are endangered. Don't promote poaching

1483. Use public transportation and car shares, if possible

1484. Consider a housing swap when traveling overseas— someone uses your place while you use his—produces a smaller carbon footprint

Workplace Kindness

1485. Invite coworkers—especially new hires—to eat lunch with you

1486. Help a new employee at your work meet other people, understand the business, find storage areas, etc. Help make a new employee feel welcome

1487. Praise coworkers when they've done a good job. Let upper management know when people are putting forth extra effort and do your part to help them advance in their careers

1488. Ask if your employer would hire nonviolent parolees for employment. These people have a very hard time finding employment

1489. Organize business-clothing drive for an organization or agency that provides clothing to people looking for work who can't afford to purchase interview/work clothes. Include shoes, briefcases, messenger bags, etc.

1490. Don't talk over people

1491. Invite your coworkers to dinner

1492. Tell a coworker you appreciate him—and mean it

1493. Don't be jealous of your coworkers when they achieve a goal—everyone in the company benefits when people do their jobs well

1494. Don't be envious of your coworkers' friendships—they all add up to a better company

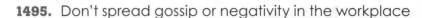

1495. Don't spread gossip or negativity in the workplace

1496. Don't let a coworker walk to her car alone in the dark

1497. With your supervisor's or manager's approval, invite a college or high school student who is interested in your field to shadow you at work for a day. Treat him or her to lunch with you and a colleague

1498. Be a secret pal and leave surprises on the desks of your coworkers

1499. Laugh with your coworkers and let them know they have a good sense of humor

1500. Compliment a coworker when he does a good job

1501. If the good job warrants a bigger thank you, email him and copy his boss and the boss's boss

1502. Offer to help when a coworker is overwhelmed—and mean it!

1503. Cross-train with your coworkers so you can help each other more efficiently

1504. Look at the photos of the children of your coworkers and find something positive to say—how beautiful their children are, what pretty eyes, what gorgeous hair— and mean it!

1505. Listen to your coworkers when they are happy and when they are sad—have an empathetic ear

1506. Don't try to outdo your coworkers when they are talking to you—if they are happy because their child came in second in the beauty contest, don't tell them your child came in first. Let them enjoy their moment!

1507. When you are making a run to the vending machine, ask your coworkers if they want anything

1508. Help a coworker clean up a spill or mess she made

1509. If a coworker is having trouble understanding a process or procedure that you understand—especially with the computer—help him

1510. Don't take credit for an idea your coworker had—give her kudos and help her make the idea work

1511. Help a coworker with heavy box or if you see them struggling with multiple packages

1512. Open the door for a coworker

1513. Show your coworker respect—don't interrupt or talk over him

1514. If the copy machine jams when you are using it, don't just walk away. Fix the jam or call the department that can help. Put a note on the copier saying when you called so others don't waste their time doing it too

1515. Help keep the common areas at work clean—clear your table after lunch, throw away trash you find, keep the bathrooms clean, etc.

1516. Smile as much as you can—most of your coworkers will smile back! If you don't feel like smiling, that's OK—no one can be "up" all the time

1517. Always show respect for your coworkers and their beliefs, their personal belongings, their space, etc. through your actions and words

1518. Welcome and get to know new employees

1519. Don't try to take away or minimize the recognition that is rightly a coworker's

1520. Praise in public and criticize in private

1521. Keep flashlights, extra canned food, etc., in your desk and let your office mates know where these things are. You never know when a natural disaster may strike or the electricity goes out

1522. If a coworker has a bowl of treats, candy, etc., to share and you take some, refill the bowl every now and then

1523. Handwrite a thank you note on stationery to a department that has helped you accomplish a task—it's a nice way to let everyone know they helped you

1524. If you bring a food dish to share at a function and people enjoy it, give them the recipe

1525. If a coworker has a death in the family, don't avoid him when he gets back to work—tell him you are so sorry and let him talk about it if they need to—don't interrupt him, just let him talk

1526. Help keep the workplace clean by throwing away trash and being respectful in the bathroom. If you spill something, clean it up well. If you use the sink, clean it

1527. If you drink coffee at the office, make a new pot every once in a while

1528. If you use a machine that needs occasional cleaning, paper replaced, water added—do it sometimes. Don't expect someone else to always do the jobs no one likes to do

1529. Hold an umbrella over a coworker who has forgotten his and walk him to his car

1530. Clear the snow and ice off the windows of all the cars in the employee parking lot

1531. Lots of people have a certain place they like to park— let your coworkers have their spot if possible, and you can find another spot

1532. If you see a the light is out (blinker, taillight, headlight, etc.) on a coworker's car, tell her so she doesn't get a ticket

1533. If you see the license plate is expired on a coworker's car, remind him to get that updated or he might get a ticket

1534. If you say you are going to keep a coworker and her family in your thoughts and prayers—do it

1535. If it's your coworker's birthday, tell him Happy Birthday! Don't ask how old he is or what he's going to do to celebrate unless you know him well

1536. If you work with people who have younger children than you do, offer them gently used toys and clothes your children have outgrown

1537. Celebrate for no other reason than to say thank you to your coworkers

1538. Give at least one compliment to at least one of your coworkers every day and mean it

1539. Offer to give your coworker a ride to or from work—even if it's not on your way—when he's having car troubles

1540. Encourage employees to invest in a beverage mug. When a new employee is hired give her a new mug

1541. Tell a coworker why you appreciate him and why

1542. Thank a coworker as soon as you can when he's done you a favor

1543. If there is a mess, clean it up—no matter who made it

1544. Thank your boss when she has helped you. Tell your boss when you think she's done a great job. Tell her you appreciate her and why

1545. Pick up trash, put things back in place, fill the paper tray of the copier, etc. Don't call attention to your actions—just do them

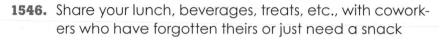

1546. Share your lunch, beverages, treats, etc., with cowork-ers who have forgotten theirs or just need a snack

1547. Start a company collection of books and stuffed ani-mals and give to the local police department to give when they go into homes to arrest a parent and there are children there

1548. Start a company collection of used luggage and donate it to a foster care service. Most foster children have no luggage to transport their belongings from one house to another and they use trash bags

1549. Start a company collection of school supplies to do-nate to a local food pantry or St. Vincent de Paul Soci-ety before school starts. Many pantries and nonprofit organizations collect the school supplies to distribute the children who have none

1550. Bring a cup of coffee, a soda, a flower—something—to a coworker who is really having a tough day or putting in a lot of overtime. Let him know you see how hard he works

1551. If your children have outgrown diapers and you have opened packages you can't use any longer, give them to someone at work with a child who can use them

1552. Don't gossip

1553. Show a coworker how to use a computer program. And have patience—it took you a while to learn it, too!

1554. Learn about the jobs of your coworkers, their responsi-bilities, when certain things are due, etc. Most people will appreciate your interest and will be happy to show you how they accomplish their tasks

1555. Respect that all workplaces change as new people are added

1556. Take the initiative and ask your supervisor if you can hire a college junior or senior student studying your field

1557. Offer to teach your job skills through a library or continuing-education program

1558. Investigate what your church has to offer in the way of workshops, etc. that are offered to people who are out of work or looking to change jobs and volunteer to help teach the workshops. If there are none, offer to organize something

1559. Volunteer to teach a course through the library or other nonprofit about your career, job-hunting skills, etc.

1560. Help an out-of-work friend network and job hunt

1561. Bring your children to your job and show them around

1562. If you can afford it, create a scholarship at your college alma mater for a student going into a specific field or with whatever criteria you wish

1563. Donate to a university of your choice and see if your employer will match your donation—many employers will match donations to colleges and universities

When a Coworker Is on Medical Leave

1564. Take pictures of people in the office waving, holding signs—whatever they think of—and enclose them in a card

1565. Send the person four or five funny cartoons

1566. Make a "What's Wrong With These Pictures?" scrapbook: Take pictures of coworkers doing things they used to do with the coworker: talking to the coworker's empty desk chair, an empty chair at staff meeting, or an empty space in the cafeteria line; having a staff meeting where everyone looks attentively toward an imaginary presenter; and hugging the air. The last page of the album should answer the question: "You're not in them!"

Business Training for Jobs in Hard Times

1567. Create a peer-training group—go to the experts—others that do that job

1568. Highlight internal talent

1569. Create your own "radio" shows, where employees answer carefully thought-out questions

1570. Implement job shadowing

1571. Create and/or expand job mentoring

1572. Develop "teachers" for specific skills throughout the company

1573. Invite community leaders to give free presentations

1574. Focus on product knowledge

1575. Resurrect job ads

1576. Cross-train

1577. Host interdepartmental conferences

1578. Give job-rotation assignments

1579. Develop training projects

1580. Create and deliver e-learning content in-house

1581. Create an online bulletin board

1582. Market the training materials you have

More Soulful on the Job

1583. Find the most creative people at work and ask for their ideas

1584. Brainstorm daily with a coworker

1585. Tape record your ideas on your commute to and from work

1586. Present your biggest challenge to a child

1587. Take your team off-site for a day

1588. Listen more carefully to your inner muse

1589. Play music in your office

1590. Go for a daily brainstorming walk

1591. Ask someone to collaborate with you on your favorite project

1592. Exercise during your lunch break

1593. Turn on a radio at random times and listen for a "message"

1594. Invite your customers and vendors to brainstorming sessions

1595. Think of five other ways to define your challenge

1596. Assign a "fun fairy" to each of your meetings

1597. Reward yourself in specific ways for small successes

1598. Introduce odd catalysts into your daily routine

1599. Get out of the office more regularly

1600. Play with fun toys in your office whenever you get stuck

1601. Take more naps

1602. Take the train, bus, subway, instead of driving to work

1603. Do some of your work in cafés

1604. Transform your assumptions into "How can I?" questions

1605. Write down as many ideas as you can in five minutes

1606. Redesign your office

1607. Take regular daydreaming breaks

1608. Dissolve turf boundaries

1609. Initiate cross-functional brainstorming sessions

1610. Arrive earlier to the office than anyone else

1611. Turn a conference room into an upbeat "think tank" room

1612. Read odd books having nothing to do with your work

1613. Block off time on your calendar for creative thinking

1614. Take a shower in the middle of the day

1615. Keep an idea notebook at your desk or in your briefcase

1616. Decorate your office with inspiring quotes and images

1617. Create a headline of the future and the story behind it

1618. Choose to be more creative

1619. Recall a time in your life when you were very creative

1620. Wander around a bookstore while thinking about a challenge

1621. Trust your instincts more

1622. Immerse yourself in your most exciting project

1623. Open a magazine and free-associate from a word or image

1624. Write down your ideas when you first wake up in the morning

1625. Ask yourself what the simplest solution is

1626. Get fast feedback from people you trust

1627. Conduct more experiments

1628. Ask yourself what the market wants or needs

1629. Ask ,"What's the worst thing that could happen if I fail?"

1630. Pilot your idea, even if it's not completely ready

1631. Work "in the cracks"—small bursts of creative energy

1632. Incubate (sleep on it)

1633. Test existing boundaries—and then test them again

1634. Schedule time with the smartest people at work

1635. Visit your customers more frequently

1636. Benchmark your competitors—then adapt their successes

1637. Involve your boss or peers in your most fascinating project

1638. Imagine you already know the answer. What would it be?

1639. Create ground rules with your team that foster new thinking

1640. Ask stupid questions. Then ask some more

1641. Challenge everything you do

1642. Give yourself a deadline—and stick to it

1643. Look for three alternatives to every solution you originate

1644. Make connections between seemingly disconnected things

1645. Use creative-thinking techniques

1646. Use Free the Genie cards (www.ideachampions.com/free_the_genie)

1647. Use similes and metaphors when describing your ideas

1648. Be sillier than usual

1649. Ask, "How can I accomplish my goal in half the time?"

1650. Take a break when you are stuck on a problem

1651. Think how your biggest hero might approach your challenge

1652. Declare Friday afternoons a "no-email zone"

1653. Ask five people how they would improve your idea

1654. Create a wall of images that inspires you

1655. Do more of what already helps you be creative off the job

1656. Laugh more, worry less

1657. Remember your dreams—then write them down

1658. Ask impossible questions

1659. Eliminate all unnecessary bureaucratic and administrative tasks

1660. Create a compelling vision of what you want to accomplish

1661. Work on your hottest project every day, even if only 5 minutes

1662. Do whatever is necessary to create a sense of urgency

1663. Go for a walk anytime you're stuck

1664. Meditate or do relaxation exercises

1665. Take more breaks

1666. Go out for lunch with your team more often

1667. Eat lunch with a different person each day

1668. Ask for forgiveness, not permission

1669. Invite an outside facilitator to lead a brainstorming session

1670. Take more risks outside of the office

1671. Take more risks inside the office

1672. Ask for help when you need it

1673. Know that it is possible to make a difference

1674. Find a mentor

1675. Find someone to mentor

1676. Acknowledge all your successes at the end of each day

1677. Create an "idea piggy bank" and make deposits daily

1678. Have shorter meetings

1679. Try the techniques in Awake at the Wheel (www.awakeatthewheel.info)

1680. Don't listen to or watch the news for 24 hours

1681. Make drawings of your ideas

1682. Think about your project or challenge before going to bed

1683. Divide your idea into components. Then rethink each part

1684. Post this list near your desk and read it daily

1685. Try to describe your idea as you would to Homer Simpson

1686. Don't leave work before you write one idea in your notebook

1687. Do research about a destination you find inspiring

Tips to Improve Self-Esteem (Yours and Others')

1688. Acknowledge strengths

1689. Don't put up with crap from yourself and others

1690. Lose negative friends

1691. Read biographies of successful people

1692. Learn to accept compliments

1693. Promote positivity

1694. Compare yourself to yourself

1695. Don't put yourself or others down

1696. It is better to be a first-rate version of yourself than a second-rate version of someone else

1697. Learn from those who have done it, not from those who talked about it

1698. Apply what you learn

1699. Set your own rules to live by

1700. Forgive yourself and others

1701. You don't know what others are thinking, so don't assume

1702. Others don't know what you are thinking, so don't assume

1703. Remind yourself we are all human and at one time or another share the same emotions

1704. Be empathetic

1705. Listen to yourself and others

1706. Become a hero

1707. Stay simple, but not stupid

1708. Work at self-improvement every day

1709. Because a self-coach

Develop Your Mind (and Others')

1710. Do the thing you fear the most

1711. Stand up for yourself

1712. Stop talking

1713. Strengthen your strengths and help others do the same

1714. Talk a walk around an art gallery

1715. Blindfold yourself and someone else, then daydream together

1716. Dance when there's nobody there

1717. Give money to someone unexpectedly

1718. Take risks and encourage others to take risks

1719. Talk to a stranger

1720. Walk around the house naked

1721. Read a book by an author you most avoid

1722. Read a banned book

1723. Write an article about yourself

1724. Write your own obituary

1725. Stop contact with your "down" people

1726. Start a group meditation

1727. Ask for a discount or give one to someone else who didn't ask

1728. Risk embarrassment

1729. Work toward what you think is an impossible goal

1730. Practice gratitude

1731. Do something nice and don't tell a soul

1732. Share your skills

1733. Write your future life story

1734. Help someone else write their future life story

1735. Give a gift for no reason

1736. Pass on your good books

1737. Forgive behavior

1738. Allow someone to compliment yourself and others

1739. Write a comment

1740. Tell your friends and colleagues how good they are

1741. With his or her permission, make a video of someone you admire and post it on You Tube

1742. List all your worries

1743. Work on each worry in turn

1744. Research successful people

1745. Tweet your moods

1746. Stop watching soaps

1747. Have a drama-free day

1748. Have a news break

1749. Daydream

1750. Stay in your pajamas all day and don't go anywhere except the bed, the bathroom, the couch, and the refrigerator

1751. Listen and follow your instincts

1752. Ask a friend about her instincts

1753. Find saved money and give it away

1754. Always admit when you made a mistake

1755. Forgive mistakes of others

1756. Do something every day to improve your mind

1757. Go fly a kite

1758. Change your thinking style

1759. Pass on your knowledge

1760. Ask for what you want in life

1761. Sing your heart out

1762. Love the one you're with

1763. Pace your studies

1764. Make new friendships

1765. Make love regularly

1766. Listen to music

1767. Have a sleep-in

1768. Look for evidence of your beliefs

1769. Travel often

1770. Tidy house, tidy mind

1771. Read philosophy

1772. Keep up with new theories

1773. Take one action toward your goals every day

1774. Help others with their goals

1775. Confront your stressors

1776. Quit bad habits

1777. Break old patterns

1778. Go to a concert

1779. Join an internet group

1780. Practice patience

1781. Practice divergent thinking

1782. Put on a new hat

1783. Stop trying to multitask

1784. Allocate time for worrying

1785. Stop hemming and hawing and just do it

1786. Read the dictionary

1787. Overdeliver on a promise

Caring for the Sick

1788. Read the Spoon Theory and send a sick friend the link (www.butyoudontlooksick.com/2009/08/the_spoon_theory.php)

1789. Don't forget she's sick!

1790. If the chronically ill person has a baby, children, or even a dog, help him with his responsibilities

1791. Don't ask "What can I do?" Volunteer to do specific tasks

1792. Don't act like a guest when you visit—don't expect the ill to pour you a cup of coffee

1793. If out-of-towners are coming to visit, offer to house the guests so the sick person doesn't have to

1794. Start a meal brigade, with each person taking a different day of the week

1795. Be flexible, never let the sick person feel guilty about things he cannot do

1796. Before you come over, ask if there is an errand you can run on your way—same thing when you leave

1797. Just listen, sometimes until it hurts, and don't say anything

1798. If it seems appropriate, get them in touch with a support group

1799. Treat her and her family to a gift of movie rentals via postal service

1800. Don't forget to invite sick people to events—they never know when they'll feel well enough to attend

1801. Understand that sick people live in a constant state of no-guarantee decision-making

1802. Encourage him to make a wishlist (online) and add anything that makes his life easier

1803. Educate yourself on the illness, but don't share what you've learned unless the sick person asks you to

1804. Research support programs for the disease in your area

1805. Don't forget about caregivers—give them a break too

1806. Be you sick friend's personal advocate

1807. Don't tell him about your sister's mother-in-law's best friend who tried a cure for the same illness and...

1808. Accept that a chronic illness may be lifelong or take your friend's life

1809. Teach her a new hobby that they always wanted to learn

1810. Never assume he's an invalid—ask before you do things for him

1811. Practice simple acts of kindness

1812. Never say "maybe you're not sick after all" or "it can't hurt that much"

1813. Always ask what time of day is a good time for a visit

1814. Simple gifts such as a book or magazine subscription can be very important gifts

1815. If she doesn't already have a cell phone, get her a simple one so she can always call for help

1816. Be sure important numbers such as yours are on the speed dials of every phone in the house

1817. Be aware that things that seem minor to you may be mountains to the sick

1818. Never tease him about how lucky he is not to have to go to work

1819. Always ask before touching, hugging, or even shaking hands—this might be very painful

1820. Extreme pain and tiredness that comes with long illness makes people cranky

1821. Never smoke around sick people

1822. Make sure she has an answering machine to screen calls

1823. Never criticize him for taking drugs that may be addictive in the long-run

1824. Encourage her to research her own disease and pro-vide the tools to help her

1825. If he needs to cry, let him

1826. Just be there

1827. Remember, that while help is always welcome, don't make her into the invalid she isn't

1828. Send cards and letters often, and have distant friends do the same

1829. If she tells you she might stop treatment, tell her you'll stand by her decision no matter what it is

Questions to Ask About Terminal Illness

1830. Can you tell me about your illness?

1831. Do you think about dying?

1832. Are you scared?

1833. How do you imagine your death?

1834. Do you believe in an afterlife?

1835. Do you regret anything?

1836. Do you look at your life differently now than you did before you were diagnosed?

1837. Do you have any last wishes?

1838. If you were to give advice to me or my children, what would it be?

1839. What have you learned from life? The most important things?

1840. Has this illness changed you? What have you learned?

1841. How do you want to be remembered?

Helping Others Deal With Grief

1842. Do not say you understand—all grief is personal

1843. Avoid clichés

1844. Acknowledge their pain

1845. Avoid telling them to be strong

1846. Look for signs of a prolonged problem

1847. Write a personal note of compassion

1848. Make yourself available

1849. Encourage the grieving person to write down his thoughts

1850. Ask what can you do

1851. Understand the importance of the loss

1852. Talk about how your past losses and how you feel about them

1853. Encourage the grieving to talk about their feelings

1854. Encourage them to talk about the loss

1855. Look at photos of the lost loved one

1856. Attend memorials

1857. Create an online memorial

1858. Compile a memory book

1859. Set up a scholarship fund in honor of their loved one

1860. Encourage them to write a eulogy reflecting the high-lights of their loved one's life

1861. Make a charitable contribution in the name of their loved one

1862. Send a card and flowers

1863. Bring a meal

1864. Check on them regularly

1865. Don't ask them to move on

1866. Pray with them and for them

Overcoming Your Own Grief

1867. Let yourself grieve

1868. Understand you are not alone in your grief

1869. Don't hold it all in

1870. Understand that not everyone experiences grief in the same way

1871. Don't be afraid or ashamed to ask for help

1872. Immerse yourself in something you enjoy

1873. Celebrate the life, not the loss

1874. Don't use your grief as an excuse for bad behavior

1875. Take one day at a time

1876. Honor the one you have lost

1877. Do not lose hope

1878. Know you can get through the grief

Friends With Broken Hearts

1879. Encourage them to begin and end their day with simple exercise such as yoga, Pilates, tai chi

1880. Help them replace the "crazy thoughts" with meditation

1881. Buy self-help books—try *The Joy of You* from Liguori

1882. Give them the gift of aroma therapy

1883. Take them to get a new haircut

1884. Draw them long, fortifying baths

1885. Let them grieve deeply and completely

1886. Buy them a gift certificate for a series of massages and make sure they go

1887. Get mad, get angry, work out the confusion with them

1888. Don't exclude them from activities—busy is good

1889. Encourage them not to contact their ex

1890. Invite them out with mutual friends

1891. Let them talk about what happened in the relationship—work it out

1892. Help them understand why they chose their ex in the first place

1893. Help them see that forgiving their ex will free them

1894. If both partners were friends, be honest and don't choose one over the other

1895. Don't take sides

1896. Create a supportive community

1897. Encourage them to join a divorce support group

1898. Buy them a journal and encourage them to write out what is important to them

1899. Don't let them play the martyr

1900. Don't bring out "the good old days" when they were married

1901. Encourage them to get professional help if needed

1902. Go shopping for something new

1903. Travel to new spaces

1904. Help them open their life to new people and experiences

1905. Encourage the kids to talk openly about what bothers them

1906. Emphasize that the divorce was not their fault

1907. Help them and their parents understand that their behavior may reflect their fear, confusion, sadness and sense of loss

1908. Encourage parents to be honest with their kids

1909. Be honest with the kids yourself

1910. Keep kids involved in all activities

1911. Encourage parents to maintain discipline and schedules

1912. Make an effort to spend quality time with the children of divorce

1913. Keep parents informed with what you are seeing in the kids

Handling Medical Emergencies

1914. Learn how to recognize emergency warning signs

1915. Stay calm

1916. Make a decision to act

1917. Better safe than sorry; call for help

1918. If poisoning is suspected (especially in children), call for help and keep evidence of the possible poison

1919. Keep a list of emergency numbers stored on your phone—police, ambulance, fire department, poison center, etc.

1920. Check for medical alert bracelets

1921. Check breathing and heartbeat—if not present, begin CPR

1922. If bleeding, use pressure on the wound

1923. Know where to get help

1924. Learn what to do until help arrives

1925. Take a first aid course prior to ever being in the situation

1926. Learn what NOT to do in an emergency

1927. Call 911

1928. If in doubt, call 911

1929. Carry a first aid kit in your car

1930. Do not move anyone who is unconscious

1931. Do not move anyone who has hit his head

1932. Do not move anyone after a traffic accident or fall

1933. Treat burns with cool water

1934. If you suspect a heart attack, get the person into a comfortable position (sometimes this is sitting up if they are having trouble breathing)—loosen clothing

Help Friends With Depression

1935. Talk about it

1936. Invite them to fun activities and encourage them to participate

1937. Start an exercise program with them

1938. Encourage them to get professional help, if needed

1939. Encourage their family to get involved in solutions

1940. Help them understand that depression is a medical condition

1941. Encourage meditation

1942. Help them set achievable goals

1943. Encourage them to set a routine and stick to it

1944. Do not invite them to drink or do drugs

1945. Get them out of the house

1946. Go organic food shopping with them

1947. Take a natural foods class together

1948. Encourage journaling

1949. Begin with small steps and don't expect the depression to disappear immediately

1950. Don't underestimate how depression impacts the individual

1951. Don't belittle and say "it's not that bad"

1952. Take an art class together—be creative

1953. Understand that depression is also physical—aches, pains and headaches

1954. Anxiety attacks go with the territory—help your friend calm down

1955. Do not become their crutch—depression can feel contagious

1956. Understand that tempers can flair—don't hold grudges

1957. Work with them to discover the source of their depression

1958. Help them learn their "triggers"

1959. Crack jokes—but not at them—laugh like mad

1960. Do not tolerate violence

Make Someone's Monday

1961. Allow someone to pull in front of you on the road on the way to work

1962. Pay for the person behind you at the coffee drive-thru

1963. Buy flowers at your grocery store and give them to the cashier on the way out

1964. Hold the elevator

1965. Be the secret Chocolate Fairy in your office—put a small piece at everyone's desk

1966. Just say please

1967. Just be YOU!

1968. Volunteer to do an unpleasant task

1969. Forward a compliment that someone else shared with you about them

1970. Really listen, and look your coworkers in the eye

1971. Pass on a compliment to their boss

1972. Thank someone for going the extra mile

1973. Get into the office 5 minutes early and have coffee made

1974. Affirm that all employees are doing important work, and we are all in it together

1975. Write a note to the boss, stating something that they did to make your job better

1976. Offer to lend a hand

1977. Instead of saying "have a nice day," say "make a great day"

1978. Smile when you answer the phone—people on the other end can tell

1979. At the end of the day, ask your coworkers: "What was the best thing you did today?"

Women Changing the World

1980. Donate a free mammogram every day to another woman

1981. Give speeches and presentations on personal experiences

1982. Join a women's blog and/or online discussion group

1983. Go to a children's zoo or park where you are allowed to feed the animals

1984. Help sort, launder, and fold clothing at an emergency shelter

1985. Join in Together We Can Change the World Day (www. togetherwecanchangetheworldday.com)

1986. Adopt the area around one of the entrances to your neighborhood and clean it up, plant flowers

1987. Start an "adopt grandparents" program at a local senior center

1988. Offer your services to help write resumés and cover letters at the local women's shelter

1989. Role play job interviews for other women seeking jobs

1990. When waiting for your number to be called at the store, trade numbers with a woman with kids

1991. Carry inexpensive pocket-sized rain ponchos and hand them out in a rainstorm

1992. Just read

1993. Volunteer to staff hotlines (you can do it from your home)

1994. Volunteer at the local hospital Pediatric Ward

1995. Celebrate Grandparents Day

1996. Teach English

1997. Donate past issues of women's magazines to a women's prison

1998. Organize a clean-up and repair day for a single mother in need

1999. Teach your kids to invite friends to a party

2000. Teach your kids to send thank-you notes

2001. Gather your women friends, and ask them to bring at least one woman friend with them for a community discussion

2002. If there isn't one, start a Neighborhood Watch

2003. If there is a Neighborhood Watch, volunteer your time

2004. Organize a spring or fall clean-up project

2005. Help fund health care for children every day

2006. Collect stuffed toy teddy bears for your local police station or trauma center

2007. Make (knit, crochet or sew) teddy bears for your local police station or trauma center

2008. Volunteer to teach a session on resumés, cover letters and interviews at a women's prison

2009. Gather a group of women to have a "Random Acts of Kindness" weekend

2010. Organize a pamphlet distribution program for a local charity

2011. Volunteer to read at hospitals and nursing homes

2012. Help repackage surplus food for food pantries, check out www.feedingamerica.org

2013. Invite a single mom and her kids to lunch

2014. Offer free babysitting for a single mom hunting for a job

2015. Go on a short-term mission project organized by your church or women's group

2016. Join the Peace Corps or AmeriCorps

2017. Create holiday baskets for families having difficult times

2018. Organize a neighborhood yard sale for charity

2019. Create scrapbooks as gifts

2020. Leave enough money in a vending machine to pay for the next person—free treats

2021. When you complete your "punch card" at a fast food restaurant or coffee shop, give it to someone on the street

2022. Create and donate floral arrangements for nursing homes

2023. Teach a free class for

2024. Act as a translator at a hospital

2025. Teach a foreign language

2026. Create a slide show of your travel experiences and volunteer to give presentations

2027. Clean out closets, basement, attic and donate your finds

2028. Send a card or e-note to a troubled friend

2029. Help preserve endangered lands

2030. At the public pool, pay the admission for an entire family

2031. Volunteer to be a chaperon at a school dance

2032. Offer to be a monitor on a school field trip

2033. Offer homework help

2034. Start a drop-in homework help center

2035. Get a group together for a food drive challenge

2036. Organize a Parents' Night Out

2037. Start a kids' star-gazing club

2038. Surprise your spouse with a candlelight dinner when he least expects it

2039. Recycle your books to local libraries, schools, nursing homes, or women's shelters

2040. Treat a friend in need to a day at the spa

2041. Gift a pedicure to a pregnant friend

Become a Body-Positive Advocate

2042. Love yourself, whatever size you are

2043. Understand that you're beautiful

2044. Let go of fear

2045. Challenge fatphobic (and thinphobic) statements when you hear them

2046. Read blogs, leave comments, join the community

2047. Bring body positivity and size acceptance issues into your communities

2048. Link to your favorite body positivity blogs, and e-mail others the link

2049. Brainstorm different ways to be an advocate

2050. Create body-positive art

2051. Have more to say or a unique perspective

2052. Start your own body positive blog

2053. Learn to accept your own body

2054. Attend and support women's conferences

2055. Form an emotional support group

Improve Your Body Image

2056. Try not to weigh yourself

2057. Really notice how you feel

2058. Try becoming more present in your own body—inside your own skin

2059. Eat mindfully—love food for its flavor and texture—not for comfort

2060. Surround yourself with positive images of women that reflect different sizes

2061. No more "negative" statements about yourself

2062. Shop for clothes that compliment the body you have

2063. Tailor clothes to fit

2064. Participate in activities you love, such as dancing, swimming, etc., without shame

2065. Exercise because it is good and helps your emotional state

2066. Remember when you were a child and felt good about your body—keep that thought

2067. Touch and be touched

2068. Treat your body gently, the way you would treat someone you love

2069. Pay attention to the things you like about your body—eyes, color of hair, etc.

2070. Make a list of all the ways your body has helped you

2071. Thank your body in a heartfelt way

2072. Listen to what you are saying

2073. Give yourself deliberate, positive messages

2074. Watch your actions and what they tell you about your attitude to your body

2075. Remember people love you, not your body—or they are not your friends

Find Joy, Fun, and Love in Your Life

2076. Really pay attention to people you might normally ignore

2077. Start a conversation with someone you might not normally talk to

2078. Learn something interesting about someone you hardly know

2079. Create rituals for yourself that are nurturing and supportive

2080. Go out to a local farm where they let you pick your own produce

2081. Have a good cry and a good laugh

2082. Scribble for ten minutes with either crayons or colored pens—don't judge it

2083. Go out in nature early in the morning and note how things look with dew on them

2084. Feed the squirrels and birds in the park

2085. Volunteer for something that never crossed your mind— maybe cleaning pens at the zoo

2086. Take a walk around your home and think about how to improve it

2087. Set butterflies, bumblebees, and lady beetles loose in the spring

2088. Use dried plants to make your own greeting cards

Men Helping Men

2089. Listen attentively to what he has to say and ask follow-up questions on subjects that are important

2090. If you notice that you have common "likes" get together and do them

2091. Make an effort to learn something about a friend's interests

2092. Be a buddy

2093. Ask opinions

2094. Let a friend know you appreciate his help

2095. Show patience when a friend is in crisis

2096. Withhold judgments

2097. Remember that November is prostate and testicular cancer month—get a checkup

2098. Help the men of tomorrow—become a Big Brother

2099. Volunteer to coach a sports team

2100. Become a mentor

2101. Engage other men in discussions about preventing domestic violence

2102. Teach your son gallantry and grace (courtesy and courage)

2103. Keep a sense of humor

2104. Live with integrity

2105. Trust yourself

2106. Volunteer to teach job skills at the local homeless veterans facility

2107. Share God's love

Teaching Skills

2108. Conduct a writing/poetry workshop for children through your local library

2109. Help your kids (and their friends) with their homework

2110. Host a foreign-exchange student

2111. Conduct a craft class at your local library for school-aged students to help them make a Father's Day gift for their dads or stepdads

2112. Apply or volunteer to teach adult continuing-education classes at the local community college or civic center

2113. Teach English to new residents

2114. Teach English overseas

2115. Start a free lecture series in your community—invite experts in every field to talk—from bird watching to physics

Be a Better Leader

2116. Volunteer to help before you know what you are really needed for

2117. Show up early for a meeting and welcome everyone with a handshake as they arrive

2118. Facilitate a meeting for someone you work with

2119. It's better to communicate really difficult stuff sooner than try to fix really difficult stuff later

2120. Prepare for a meeting before you attend and present your thoughts on the meeting topics first

2121. Highlight several strengths or skills you see another person has and tell them

2122. Tell stories of times where you have learned something new from a failure

2123. Display or publish your own personal values to your coworkers

2124. Introduce yourself to anyone you don't know in the workplace

2125. Get to know one of your colleagues outside of the work setting

2126. Develop and use a consistent positive response to greetings like, "Hi, how are you?"

2127. Share with someone one of your vulnerabilities

2128. Always treat others respectfully

2129. Outline for your boss each month all your accomplishments, plans and lessons learned

2130. Make calls to maintain your network and to keep your contacts informed of your presence and lend an offer of help should they need it

2131. Be transparent and share personal stories

2132. Provide regular feedback to others about behaviors and actions you can see and hear

2133. Share your vision

2134. Dream big

2135. Define, build and maintain your reputation

2136. Spend more time with those performing well than those not

2137. Leave no footprints on your face or on anyone else's

2138. Bend with the times, bend with people, but don't bend your standards and ethics

2139. Keep business performance and expectations independent of any personal relationship (business is business and personal is personal)

2140. Communicate clearly, inquire deeper and paraphrase often

2141. Spend time communicating with people in private

2142. Ask about and learn what motivates other people to help them achieve it

2143. Start an informal learning time at lunch with colleagues and pick various topics to cover on a regular schedule

2144. Send an e-mail of your favorite learning websites

2145. Tell others how you learn new skills

2146. Offer to help someone develop an area you are already familiar with

2147. Teach a skill you have learned to others

2148. Learn the DiSC profile (or another type of behavior/ personality profile) to help describe and communicate more effectively with others

2149. Put at least one thing into action from every course/ book you ever complete

2150. Show empathy and compassion to others

2151. Find a mentor to help you focus your development

2152. Mentor someone else in an area or role you excel at

2153. Create/write your own training manual and share it with others

2154. Write down all of your goals with end dates and ensure they are measurable

2155. Write your desired legacy or epitaph

2156. Increase communication by using open ended questions

2157. Actively pursue and encourage continuous improvement for yourself and others

2158. Continue to grow and raise your expectations over time

2159. Accept responsibility for your own actions and make that point known

2160. Smile at the first people you see each and every day

2161. Complete the one thing you have procrastinated on the most before anything else

2162. Start procrastinating on things a leader doesn't do

2163. Encourage and promote change

2164. Add enthusiasm and passion to your presentations

2165. Say no to unimportant requests

2166. Bring up and engage in a difficult subject or conversation

2167. Keep your actions and decisions aligned with your values

2168. Read books and share them with others

2169. Be first to demonstrate and practice the Golden Rule

2170. Choose to promote someone else's idea over your own

2171. Pick three low-value things you can stop doing, and stop doing them from now on

2172. Listen and think more than you talk

2173. Show appreciation and thanks to others

2174. Be bold in your actions

2175. Overcome your biggest fear by facing it

2176. Read *Good to Great* by Jim Collins

2177. Step up your business attire a notch and keep it that way

2178. Memorize and share your favorite leadership quotes

2179. Be persistent

2180. Do one new leadership action every day

2181. Maintain and uphold professional ethics

2182. Practice what you preach

2183. Be confident in your abilities and decisions

2184. Strengthen your unique attributes

2185. Work hard and play hard

2186. Show your ability to balance work and play

2187. Let go of perfectionism for yourself and others

2188. Take initiative

2189. Reduce and even eliminate things that are distracting

2190. Set time aside for planning and strategy

2191. Review and recap your progress and accomplishments

2192. Take a day off work to volunteer for a nonprofit group

2193. Always give credit to those you work with or who work for you

2194. Don't judge others; offer help to promote change instead

2195. Be open-minded to other people's ideas and opinions

2196. Stay calm and control emotional outbreaks in all situations

2197. Sacrifice your own time or personal goal to help achieve a collective goal

2198. Take on a task or trade a task for one that no one else wants to do

2199. Contribute free of charge to personal and career development systems like wikis, blogs, articles, interviews, speaking opportunities or other related systems

2200. Find your own passions and connect with others in a community who share that passion

2201. Engage in a conversation with a stranger

2202. Keep complacency at bay and drive through resistance from others

2203. Let go of having things done your way and accept alternative paths

2204. Let others share their opinions before you

2205. Express gratitude and appreciation for what you have

2206. Put love into what you do and how you do it

2207. Build trust by offering to trust people before expecting it to be earned

2208. Rely on and reveal your spiritual guidance that helps you be the leader you are

2209. Make decisions that build a team, not an individual

2210. Do the right thing even if it won't be liked

2211. Give first and without any expectation

2212. Be humble and willing to serve others

Take Care of a Caregiver

2213. Pick up an inexpensive bouquet of flowers and give them to a caregiver

2214. If a friend takes in a homeless pet, give him or her a bag of pet food; better yet, throw a pet-supply shower with other friends

2215. If a friend takes in someone else's children, throw a shower to help him or her load up on toiletries, nonperishable snacks, school supplies, and other needed items

2216. Help caregivers find and apply for low- or no-cost programs that can help you or a loved one stay healthy, cover basic expenses (such as food, home heating, medical care, or prescription drugs), assist older relatives, and support children in your care

2217. Give the caregiver a day off—hire in help

2218. Ask if you can run errands for a caregiver

2219. Give a gift certificate to a day at the spa

2220. Don't leave caregivers out function just because they will probably say no

2221. Be supportive

Caregiver Protection

2222. Laugh about something every day

2223. Take care of yourself physically

2224. Eat a well-balanced diet

2225. Talk with someone every day

2226. Let family and friends help. Give them printed material on memory disorders so they can better understand your relative. Give them a chance

2227. Give yourself permission to have a good cry. Tears aren't a weakness, they reduce tension

2228. Exercise—a brisk walk counts

2229. Get adequate rest

2230. Try a bowl of Cheerios and milk before bed to promote sleep

2231. Avoid noisy and/or tension-filled movies at night. The late news itself can add to stress—skip it

2232. Reduce daily caffeine intake

2233. Get professional help if you feel your support system isn't adequate or if you feel overwhelmed

2234. Take a break every day, even if it's only 10 minutes alone in the backyard

2235. Explore community resources and connect yourself with them

2236. Listen to music

2237. Learn relaxation techniques

2238. Regularly attend one or more support groups and education workshops

2239. Give yourself a treat at least once a month: an ice cream cone, a new shirt or dress, a night out with friends, a flowering plant

2240. Read your Caregiver's Bill of Rights (and *Today's Caregiver* magazine). Know your limitations

With My Compliments

2241. Compliment someone on something you think he or she hears all the time (just because someone has beautiful hair doesn't mean anyone ever says it)

2242. Compliment someone on something everyone takes for granted, like how cleverly they've decorated their office or how they always know what to say at an awkward moment

2243. If someone says something nice to you about a coworker, repeat it to the coworker—third-party compliments are the best

2244. When you're in public and you see well-behaved children, compliment their parents

The Giving Game

2245. If you get a valuable coupon for something you can't use, take it to work and put it on the bulletin board

2246. If you get a gift card you can't use, donate it to a charity to use for fundraising or employee appreciation days

2247. In place of a walkathon, bike-a-thon, dance-a-thon, and the like, consider holding a service-a-thon as a more purposeful fundraiser

2248. Contribute to the Heifer Project at www.Heifer.org

2249. Loan money through a group such as KIVA at www.Kiva.org

2250. If there is a sick coworker that is running out of sick leave or vacation time, give them some of your time

2251. Set aside a portion of pay check for your favorite charity

2252. Leave a portion of your estate to your favorite charity

2253. Give your old car, boat, motorcycle, even your house to a fund-raising auction

2254. Make a pact to buy nothing new for one year. Calculate the money you saved and give it to your favorite charity

2255. Save all your pennies for a year, and give them to a charity

2256. Donate your winnings from an in-office pool to charity

2257. Commit your bonus or yearly salary increase to a charity

2258. Buy gift cards at popular food chains and give them to the homeless who may solicit you for change

2259. Set up an emergency fund for coworkers in need

2260. Donate regularly to your house of worship

2261. Donate to Toys for Tots

2262. Be a secret Santa

2263. Set up trust funds for nieces and nephews who are less fortunate, and challenge your siblings to do the same

2264. Start a family fund for family emergencies

Volunteer Your Time

2265. Visit a retirement home on a regular basis and listen to the residents' stories. Take notes and write their history

2266. When a clerk, waiter/waitress, or receptionist gives exceptional service, make sure you let their supervisor know about this. Make the extra effort to find a manager and relate your experience. It takes as much time to offer praise as it does to complain!

2267. Volunteer to read to children at the library

2268. Participate in the annual "Relay for Life" which benefits cancer research

2269. Gather a group of friends and make lap blankets for residents of a nursing home. Share the cutting tasks and create the blankets as a group or have each person take several for "home work"

2270. Find a space or help to staff a thrift store in an area where it is needed. You can place ads on local religious websites, in diocesan newspapers, or in church bulletins. You will also need a drop-off place for items and volunteers to pick up items and then arrange them in the store

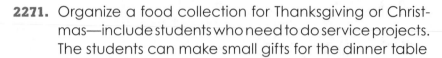

2271. Organize a food collection for Thanksgiving or Christmas—include students who need to do service projects. The students can make small gifts for the dinner table

2272. Assemble a group of family and friends to sing Christmas carols in your neighborhood or at nursing homes. Be sure to call ahead to schedule a time when residents will be able to attend

2273. Often nursing homes will take the initiative to provide cookies and drinks

2274. Ask family members and friends to spend part of Thanksgiving and Christmas serving meals at a local soup kitchen. Some places may have an early breakfast and a dinner time on these special holidays

2275. Organize a group of family, friends and coworkers to sponsor a homeless person who is ready to reenter the work force. Collect money to put toward a deposit on an apartment

2276. Collect donations to help develop a website for small charitable organizations, then organize volunteers to help with the site. This will be a great learning experience for adults and teens alike

2277. Encourage your company to support a food bank in your area and conduct several food collections throughout the year. Usually food banks need additional items during Thanksgiving and Christmas and then an additional collection for school lunch items when children return to school

2278. Every day for one week pray for a person or family in need or for a special intention

2279. Offer to host a scout troop or class field trip to visit your work, especially if it is a manufacturing plant or museum, anything children love to visit. Give the tour yourself and be attentive—you might start a young person on a career path just because of the time you spent telling them about your profession

2280. Volunteer to teach Junior Achievement in your local school

2281. Volunteer to help Catholic Charities or other nonprofits to provide job training, help with writing resumés, etc.—whatever you do best—to people needing help

Nurture Talent

2282. Volunteer at your school or parish to put together a committee to organize a talent show for the children at the school or parish. Have tryouts, make sure there are parameters on what can be performed. Charge a small fee for each act, give the winners a prize, and donate the rest back to school or church

2283. If you have experience and are good at a certain sport, volunteer to coach a child's sports team and open it up to everyone

2284. If you are artistic, volunteer to teach children or adults in your parish fundamentals of art and have the final project be to do a mural or something nice one wall in the church hall or school

2285. If you are artistic, volunteer to teach a class for the local nursing home or elder care center

2286. If you are musically talented, volunteer to help the band or choir teach at your local school. Volunteer to lead children's choir at your parish. Volunteer to teach music lessons to people who can't pay for it

2287. If you are artistically talented, organize a group of scouts, children from school, VBS children, etc., and clean up the neighborhood. While you do that, keep the things you can use to make unique art. Show the children how recycled trash can be made into beautiful artwork and let them keep their masterpieces

2288. If you are good with electronics and sound systems, volunteer to run the lights, sound system, etc. at church/school, especially if there is a children's theater group

2289. Volunteer to help organize and run a children's theater group in your school/parish. Organize a trip to a local play/musical production so the children can experience theater from the audience. Many children have never been to a play, recital, opera, etc.

2290. If you can afford it, offer a scholarship at your local Catholic school or institution of higher education to a student to exhibits a special talent—you can pick

2291. Talents come in many forms—athletic talent, singing talent, dancing talent, writing talent, etc. Make it your lifetime commitment to compliment and encourage talent wherever you see it. That means in a child, in a sibling, in a coworker, etc. Don't hesitate to let them know you see how special they are

Support the Writer

2292. Read—fall in love again with the written word

2293. Go to readings of new works

2294. Offer support and genuine criticism; that is, not criticism to make you feel better but that you think can actually help the writer. Tell the writer the things you liked and what you thought wasn't working

2295. If you know a writer, ask what he or she is working on

2296. Don't judge a writer's success or failure by the monetary standard alone

2297. Encourage children to write stories about anything and everything

2298. If you have a writer in your family or close to you, allow them the time and space to do the work. A writer needs time alone without interruption

2299. If the writer wants to discuss the work, wonderful! If not, don't press it. Some writers would rather not talk until it's finished; others like to talk about the process

2300. Know that few works ever appear fully developed in the first version Allow for the process Don't judge a writer on his or her first draft

2301. Encourage the writer to keep going

2302. Join a reading group, not just of popular or classical books, but include the work of your local writers

2303. Join and support any local or national artists' group that is, in turn, supporting the writer

2304. Donate to organizations such as The MacDowell Colony that offers residencies to writers. Often these donations are tax deductible

2305. Help the writer believe in her or himself

2306. Validate that writers are doing something of importance for our society because they are

2307. Read Shelley's *In Defense of Poetry* if you need to clarify why we need the arts

Support the Painter

2308. Tour your local galleries. Discover the world of the painter's imagination, which in turn will lead you on a journey into your own sensibilities

2309. Visit or revisit museums and rediscover your love of this art

2310. Talk with the painter and offer your encouragement and/or criticism, but always in terms of what will help the painter grow

2311. Buy a painting. Painters have to pay their bills, like all of us, and you will have something you cherish, not simply another manufactured print

2312. Validate the painter as an important member of society. Art is the statement of your culture in your time. It carries on the sensibility of your society

2313. Don't judge the painter by monetary success

2314. If you can offer a space for a painter to work, do. All painters need work space

2315. Discuss the work with the painter if he and/or she want to discuss it

2316. Donate or offer support to any organization, which is, in turn, providing vital services to the painter

2317. Encourage and give emotional/psychological support whenever you can

2318. Encourage young people to paint and to study the classics

2319. Nurture the natural instinct in all to create

2320. If the painter opens his or her studio or work place to the public, attend It will nurture you as much as the artist

2321. If you have a painter in your life, allow them the time and privacy to work

Support the Musician

2322. Listen to their music

2323. Give their music respect and attention

2324. Talk with the musician, offering encouragement and support

2325. Discuss problems with the work if the musician wants to have such a discussion

2326. Musicians often form groups of play for each other or friends/music lovers; join one. It's great fun

2327. Listen to all music; don't be limited by one genre or intimidated by classical

2328. Donate or offer support to any organization, which, in turn, is providing support for the musician

2329. If you have a musician in your life, allow him or her the time and space to work

2330. Offer the musician work space if you can

2331. Encourage young people to make their own music in whatever form they choose

2332. Validate the musician as an important member of society

2333. If the musician has CD's or is selling the music in some form, buy it

2334. Realize that the creative process might be noisy. Don't let a banging piano create hostility

2335. Most people love music; share your love with the creators of music

2336. Pay for instrument insurance for a musician

2337. If someone is playing on the street, put money in their jar and thank them for the entertainment

2338. Send kids to music camp

Support the Actor

2339. Validate that their talent exists and is worthy of time and commitment

2340. Go to any plays or readings or film projects the actor is involved in—you'll have fun

2341. Open a discussion with the actor about his or her current project, regardless the level of development. Ask the actor what he or she thought the strengths or weaknesses of a work might be

2342. If there is a theater group in your community, attend

2343. If possible, give financial support to theaters or groups that are in turn providing acting opportunities

2344. If you have a business and the actor needs time off for an audition, work with the actor so he or she can make the audition

2345. Encourage young people to form theater groups or attend the theater

2346. Plays often have readings or forums for works in progress. Actors often get their start in such a venue. Attend the readings; you'd be surprised how much fun you can have

2347. With few exceptions, acting is often without financial reward. If you can, offer some support for the actor in the knowledge that it is a craft as important as any other

2348. Simply tell the actor how much you appreciate his or her talent and achievement

Break a Habit

2349. Be aware it is a negative behavior and how it is affecting you and those in our life

2350. Visualize your life without the habit. Make the improvement in your life real for yourself

2351. Create a specific goal. Example: I want to weigh 110 pounds

2352. Create specific steps to reach that goal. Example: I can only eat 1,000 calories a day

2353. Give yourself a realistic deadline. Break that up into smaller deadlines if need be. For example: I want to lose 50 pounds. To do that, I want to lose 5 pounds a month

2354. What is the very first thing you must do to break this habit? Example: I want to stop smoking. What aids exist to help with that? Must you get rid of all the cigarettes and paraphernalia to do this? Be realistic and specific

2355. Develop a plan to cope with the setbacks and temptations that will come. Example: How will you deal with not losing weight one week when you did before and changed nothing in your eating habits?

2356. Be consistent. Don't say to yourself, "It's only this one time," because soon you will be back to your bad habit on a daily basis

2357. Substitute something healthy for the unhealthy activity. Example: instead of lighting a cigarette, take a short walk

2358. Don't be afraid to ask the people in your life for support. Example: if you want to stop smoking, ask your friends for supportive behavior. You might not wish to watch someone else smoking or eating sweets or getting high

2359. Know you can break this habit. Know that you were born with the inner strength to walk away from self-destructive behavior

2360. How will you deal with it when, once the habit is broken, and time passes—a year or two years and you again feel the strong temptation to go back?

2361. Have a "quiet time" in your life to communicate with the higher part of yourself; the spirit can always rise above. Allow yourself the time and place to know that spirit again

2362. Go back to your spiritual center of gravity as often as you need to

2363. Ask yourself what is behind this habit. If you can't confront whatever that is, the behavior may simply slip into another arena

2364. But don't expect miracles of yourself—a little each day. Remember the song: "Live one day at a time" or if need be, one minute at a time

2365. Make the changes you can each day; don't expect to move Mount Everest overnight

2366. Reward yourself when you reach goals

Work With a Toxic Boss

2367. Identify the problem behavior. Is the boss a control freak, a putdown artist, a passive-aggressive manipulator?

2368. Separate the boss's behavior from your own personal problems. Example: you may overreact to a control freak if you're a control freak yourself

2369. First, realize what you can change in your own behavior that may be contributing to the problem. Example: If the boss is anxiety-ridden and reacts by putting down the staff, are you feeding the problem by pointlessly going to the boss with your own anxiety?

2370. Stay professional. Concentrate on your job. Don't allow your own feelings of anger and resentment to dominate. Example: If the boss screams that you did not do this or that, ask the boss to be specific. If the task was not done, explain why and acknowledge your mistake. If you did the task, ask the boss to review the work

2371. Don't be submissive and fearful because it will encourage toxic behavior in the boss. Bullies get worse if no one stands up to them. However, the worker must walk a delicate line here. Keep it professional, not personal

2372. Documentation. Take clear and regular notes on the workplace. Include time, work assignment, any other people involved and feedback. Stay specific

2373. Ask for a face to face with your boss to resolve problems. In that meeting, stay calm and specific. Only do this if you think there's a possibility it will help. That depends entirely on the specific situation

2374. Try the halo effect. Tell the boss how you feel he or she does a good job. This does not mean you have to lie

2375. Focus on those things you feel the boss may do well and congratulate him or her on that behavior. Most bosses have the job because they have contributed to the company; find out what that specific contribution has been and let the boss understand you appreciate his/her unique talent

2376. The boss/employee relationship is, finally, another human relationship. The boss appears to have more power because he or she may control whether you get a paycheck (and that's power), but the boss is also answering to somebody, and to make a good accounting he or she needs the productive forces of the worker (meaning you). Use your people skills to try to bring the relationship back into a realistic balance. If the boss is having a good day, note why. It may not always be related to the workplace, but if it is, note the dynamics that day. If something always sets the boss off, can it be avoided or modified?

2377. Don't expect the boss to change, but is it possible to bring down the volume?

2378. Know the trigger points for the toxic behavior. Does he/she always yell an hour before a certain deadline? Does he/she always take it out on employees after a board meeting? If any of those trigger points can be controlled or modified, do way more than you normally would to reduce the effect on the boss

2379. If all else fails, find another job. To explain why you left your previous job, simply say you saw the company going in a different direction than the boss and the visions were not compatible, so you moved on. If you were only on the job with the toxic boss a short time, leave it off your resumé

How to Get Along With Coworkers

2380. Getting along too well with coworkers can be a problem as well as not getting along with them. Too much good cheer may distract you from work; negative relations may also affect the work

2381. Identify the coworkers who are creating the problem. If it really is that you're all having more fun being with one another than working, simply talk with your coworkers and set up times outside of work to enjoy one another's company. However, if the problem is a negative "vibe" in the workplace, identify which coworkers are contributing to that

2382. Identify the behavior. What exactly is the coworker doing?

2383. Be cooperative but not a pushover. If you can short-fuse behavior before it happens, do. Example: Coworker gets angry each time you hand over a request from the boss. Ask the coworker how she/he would like you to deal with the request. If the coworker is irrational and demanding the impossible, state your case and stay professional

2384. Greet your coworkers in the morning. A pleasant cheerful good morning can be very productive

2385. Avoid office politics. Human relationships are politics, and you will probably spend more time with those in your office than with your family, so there will always be some political aspects. But avoid the obvious pitfalls like cliques and nasty gossip or a shared negative behavior like always getting to the office late

2386. Congratulate and encourage a coworker when the job is well done

2387. If there is an issue that must be resolved between you and another worker, be as specific and professional as possible. Make sure it stays a work issue, not a personal issue

2388. Avoid putting your personal life too much into the workplace, such as spending too much time on the phone to wife and kids or partner or sharing details that are too personal for a professional environment. We're all human and some sharing of lives is natural. But if there are sensitive areas, don't assume a coworker is a lifelong friend or psychologist

2389. Treat your coworker as you wish to be treated

2390. Don't talk behind a coworker's back about the things you don't like about him or her

2391. Don't throw them under the bus to further your own aspirations. Most of this is common-sense social skills but hard to control under the pressure of the work environment. Decent human behavior has similar rules, and most of us know what those rules are: treat others as you wish to be treated; don't sabotage somebody else; don't indulge in behavior at the cost of someone else

2392. Be a team player. Think in terms of the team and what will help get the job done to the best of each member's ability

2393. Monitor yourself and others. If negative behavior is escalating, note why and who is contributing and how you can diffuse the situation. If positive behavior is growing, reinforce it. If a specific problem has developed with a coworker, take specific and professional notes

2394. Consider a face-to-face discussion with your boss about the problem; however this is not in terms of "telling on someone" or "blaming someone else." This meeting should be about how to solve the work problem, not how to get rid of someone. This is advised only when the problem really is threatening the life of the company

Support Your Library

2395. Use the library, browse all the collections, become familiar with the building and the wealth of material there

2396. Check out books (and CDs and books on tape and music)—all of it is there and free

2397. Respect the rules of the library on return policy and deadlines

2398. Respect the materials you do check out—don't bend down pages or mark in books and return the materials as you received them so that others may also enjoy their use

2399. Be quiet in the library—people are there to read or study or browse. It is not a place for conversations or telephone calls. Step outside if you want to talk on the phone

2400. Turn off your cell phone when entering the library

2401. Give to your library fund

2402. Volunteer time to your library

2403. Attend a program or event offered by the library

2404. Organize a venue around your interest and the library

2405. Underwrite an exhibit or event

2406. Make a gift to the library in honor of a loved one or associate or cause

2407. Sign up to receive email or snail mail alerts and information from your library

2408. Let your legislators know the importance of the library for your community

2409. Encourage the young people in your life to go to the library. Go with them to help them explore the cultural riches that are available there

2410. Be polite and courteous to the staff

2411. Encourage anybody of any age to go to the library. Many may not be aware of the riches a library can provide

2412. Make your legislator aware of your support for the library and its importance to your community

2413. Donate your used books or CDs or tapes to the library

2414. Buy used books often on sale at the library—they are invariably a great bargain

2415. The great library system of this country is at the heart of its democracy. Do all you can to hand it down to the next generation

Spiritual Space

2416. Keep a spiritual journal for a specified period of time. If a year seems too long, keep a journal for the season of Advent or Lent. Suggestions for journaling are available in *Advent and Christmas Wisdom* from Thomas Merton and *Lent and Easter Wisdom* from Thomas Merton

2417. Each day set aside 10 minutes (start with a kitchen timer if necessary) and enjoy one of God's creations

2418. Use your eyes—spend 10 minutes watching the clouds and seeing figures or pictures in them

2419. Use your ears—find a quiet place away from people, close your eyes, and listen to the birds and the sound of the wind

2420. Use your sense of smell—sit outside a bakery and see if you can identify what is in the oven. Appreciate it! (Savor it!)

2421. Use your sense of smell—sit outside your house or in a park and enjoy the fragrance of the flowers or the smell of freshly mowed grass

2422. Use your sense of smell and sight—visit a florist and appreciate the many shades of one color (all the reds and pinks!)

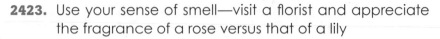
2423. Use your sense of smell—visit a florist and appreciate the fragrance of a rose versus that of a lily

2424. Organize a support group to aid single parents in spiritual matters

2425. Offer babysitting services while the parent attends church services or makes a retreat

2426. Offer to take children to Mass or church services when their parent has to work or is unable to attend due to illness

2427. Organize a group of friends, coworkers or members of your church to send care packages to new college students. Make a list of inexpensive items that can be purchased or donated and treats that can be made by the volunteers. Include an inspirational book or pamphlet as Liguori Publications' *Preparing Your Faith For College, Believe in Yourself,* or *Keeping the Faith*

2428. Add something inspirational to every e-mail as "have a blessed day" or "have a peaceful day" or "may God continue to bless you"

Capture Images

2429. If you have photography skills and equipment, offer to help a teacher, scout leader, nonprofit youth program, etc. teach children about the fundamentals of photography

2430. Take photos at your child's sporting events and make a scrapbook for your child documenting her years in the sport

2431. Take photos at your child's sporting events of some of the other players and give a copy to their parents

2432. Take photos at your child's sporting events and put together a little scrapbook of the season, have all the children sign it, and present it to the coach as a thank you for coaching

2433. If your child's team wins the tournament or does something very special, take a team photo and submit it, with all the information, to the local newspaper

2434. Go through family photos and put together a scrapbook of the different generations. Make copies of the photos and give a copy to each of your siblings, cousins, etc. Identify every photo you can! Involve your children and tell them about the people you know in the photos and family stories

2435. You take videos of your children all the time—get them out every once in a while and watch them together—your kids will love it and you will be reminded—once again—how fast time flies and how fast your children are growing up

2436. Get out the old family home movies and slides and watch them with your family. Take them to a photo place and get them converted to a DVD with music and a nice presentation. Make copies and give them as gifts to siblings, parents, cousins, etc.

2437. When your children have friends over, take photos of them playing together and give a copy to the friend's parent

2438. If you are a member of an organization, volunteer to be the historian and take photos of activities and events and put together a scrapbook/visual presentation each year to share with the group

2439. Offer to help an elderly relative go through his collection of family photos. Ask about each one and identify the people in the photos for future generations

2440. Give your children their own disposable camera while on vacation and let them take photos of things that are important to them. Help them put together a scrapbook of the vacation and it's theirs to keep

2441. If your child shows an interest in photograph, get them books from the library about it, as well as picture books of famous photographers. If you can afford it, look into signing them up for photograph lessons for children at the local community college—or maybe the local photography studio offers classes

2442. Send out yearly photos of your children/family with your Christmas cards. Friends and relatives love getting updated photos of your family. Save the ones your friends and relatives send you and put together a little album of the photos and send it back to the child in the photo to keep

2443. Take photos at family gatherings Be the self-appointed family photographer of uncles, aunts, cousins, etc. Give them copies of good photos (and destroy the bad photos). Put together a video presentation to show at family gatherings. Put together a photo album to have out at family gatherings so everyone can see them

2444. Volunteer to organize a photography contest for children. Set up different categories and foster their love of photography. Give little prizes to the winners. Work with a local business to display the entries

2445. Donate your unused photography equipment to a nonprofit agency that provides equipment to youth programs

2446. Volunteer to raise money for a charity of your choice by taking photos of owners and their pets, charging a small fee. Children could help with this and have a great time

2447. Volunteer to make—or have made—some wooden-cut outs for your parish picnic where people can stick their head in a hole and it looks like their face is on the head of a monkey or something silly like that

2448. Volunteer to take photos of the teachers/staff at school and have the photos framed and hung in the halls/classrooms at the beginning of each school year. This helps the students to learn everyone's name and it makes the teachers/staff feel special

Crafty for a Cause

2449. If you sew, ask the local hospital if they have a sewing committee you could join to make baby blankets or hats for newborns at the hospital

2450. Ask your church if they have a sewing committee you could join to make baby blankets or other items for newborns in the parish

2451. If you crochet or knit, ask your parish or local retirement facility if you could volunteer to make afghans to donate to the elderly in the parish or at the nursing home

2452. Organize a fund-raiser for your parish and recruit other people to make afghans, blankets, etc. and sell them to parishioners and then donate back to the parish

2453. Volunteer to teach sewing skills to a local scout troop to help them get a badge and foster their love of sewing

2454. Donate your old sewing equipment to a nonprofit agency that offers training to people to teach them how to sew

2455. If you quilt, offer to donate a quilt to a raffle at school or church to help make money for the organization

2456. If you quilt, offer to teach a free class at school or church to teach the children how to quilt

2457. If you quilt, offer to teach a free class to adults in your parish. By the end of the class, complete a quilt and give it to the pastor in the parish as a gift

2458. Offer to make baby clothes, blankets, hats, etc. for new babies who are born in the parish. Organize a committee to take new things to families in the parish who have newborns

2459. Organize a committee at church to make Christmas ornaments and volunteer to decorate the rectory, lobby at school, vestibule at church, etc.

2460. Volunteer to make Christmas ornaments and decorations for shut-ins in the parish and deliver them before Christmas. Offer to help decorate their home or bedroom with the items

2461. Volunteer to make Christmas ornaments and decorations for a local nursing home and deliver them before Christmas. Offer to help decorate the lobby or some of the rooms of the people who live there

2462. Organize a committee at church to make Christmas decorations and ornaments to donate to the St. Vincent de Paul Society for needy families so they can have some decorations at Christmas time

2463. Volunteer to help a teacher make preparations for a class craft project

2464. At a teen party, create a batch of fleece lap blankets and delivery to a nursing home

2465. Make afghans, quilts, mittens, hats—whatever you can— to donate to needy families. It's tough to celebrate Christmas when you are so very cold!

2466. Volunteer to help a nonprofit agency alter clothes that have been donated for people who are unemployed and interviewing for jobs

2467. Volunteer to help a nonprofit agency that collects used prom dresses (for girls who can't afford their own dresses). Offer to alter the dresses to fit the girls

2468. If you have left over felt, yarn, other craft supplies, etc., donate them to your school's art department or to the local Cub Scout or Girl Scout troop

2469. Organize a committee to start a craft fair at your school or parish. This takes work but craft fairs are usually very successful—you charge a fee to rent the booth to other crafters and you can also ask each crafter to donate something and you can sell raffle tickets for people to win the donated items

2470. If you are crafty at making greeting cards, volunteer your talents at school and during Teacher Appreciation Week. Volunteer to make a card of appreciation for each teacher and staff member

2471. Volunteer your talents at a nonprofit agency that exposes youngsters to new ideas and things—especially if you are good at leather crafting, decorating plates, model building, etc.—things they may not experience otherwise but that they might really enjoy—and maybe even make a living doing some day

Good Sportsmanship

2472. Show your support for the team! It's fun watch your children, nieces, nephews, godchildren, friends, and grandchildren play in youth sporting events. They love to be cheered on, and it gives them confidence!

2473. Practice good sportsmanship and set a good example for the children and other spectators

2474. Don't yell negative comments at the children on either team. It is best not to yell anything at all, because you may distract both the children and the other spectators

2475. Don't criticize the coach's decisions or yell at the coach If you have a questions or comment, wait until after the game to speak to them in private

2476. Don't criticize or yell at the officials. In many leagues, such as CYC and local county or city leagues, the officials are teenagers, and you should never yell at or criticize a child. Set an example by your behavior.

2477. Remember that no matter how old the official may be, he or she has the power in the game and can—and should—throw disruptive spectators out of the park

2478. Weather can be very hot or very cold—and everything in between—for soccer and baseball seasons. If it's hot, bring and set a canopy and invite other spectators under the shade. In the winter, bring an extra blanket for the person who didn't realize how cold it gets watching a soccer game in October!

2479. If there is a sign that asks you not to bring you own refreshments, obey the request and purchase your refreshments from the concession stand

2480. Many concessions stands serve alcohol. Don't drink too much and lose your self control—and self respect.

2481. If you can afford it, offer to purchase an icy or slushy for each child on your team at the concession stand after the game

2482. If you can bring your own refreshments (or you are watching a practice when the concession stand isn't open) and it's hot, bring a cooler of inexpensive, frozen popsicles and share with all the children after the game/practice

2483. Bring an extra chair when you go to watch a sporting event. Often times there isn't enough room on the bleachers, and someone else may need to borrow a chair

2484. Be sure to discard your trash at events. Most athletic associations do not hire cleaning crews but depend upon spectators cleaning up after themselves

2485. Bring extra sunscreen and bug spray to games/practices and share with other parents/children who forget to bring these items

2486. Offer to help coach if there aren't enough coaches at the game. This is especially helpful in baseball/softball where you need a third base coach and a first base coach. An older sibling can also volunteer to help the team in this way

2487. If you have staked out a shady spot to watch the game and you see someone elderly or a family with a baby, invite them to share the shade or give it up for that game

2488. If you know it's going to be a hot game, bring a cooler of ice water and several towels and put this in the dugout for the kids. Let them dip the towels in the cold water and put these on their heads, necks, etc.

Teach Kids About Sports

2489. Parents are the most important influence in a child's view of fairness

2490. Remember, competition is not "good" or "bad," but it is how it is managed that matters

2491. More isn't necessarily better

2492. Teach children to cultivate positive relationships with teammates and fellow athletes

2493. Foster healthy competition, not rivalry

2494. If it's not fun, something is wrong. Make it fun!

2495. Physical and emotional stress goes with training and competition. Teach your children to manage it

2496. Empower your child's self esteem through sports

2497. Create positive memories

Older Folks Might Need Your Help—Give It!

2498. Check in on elderly neighbors, family, friends, etc. and make sure their air conditioners/furnaces are working Offer to check the filters and replace if necessary

2499. If something isn't working or if they can't afford the utility bills, offer to make the call to a repair person. If it costs too much, offer to call their church or local city/ county agency that is set up to help elderly with heating and cooling bills

2500. Partner with a friend to visit a nursing home, where you can hand out gift packets together. Call ahead to find out what the residents need. Also, request the number of residents and the best time to visit

2501. As people get older, they have a harder time washing and styling their hair, trimming their nails, etc. Offer to give a manicure or pedicure (if you are comfortable with that) or offer to take them to a salon or barber shop to get it done

2502. Organize a committee at your church that periodically checks on the elderly members of the congregation to make sure they are OK and comfortable

2503. Organize fund-raisers to have money available when you hear someone needs a home repair or to replace an appliance. Write grant proposals to get more money to help

2504. Go to an assisted-living facility and get a list of folks who do not get visitors. Then visit them each week

2505. Donate fans in the summer to your local utility company for distribution

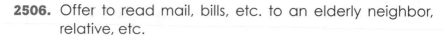

2506. Offer to read mail, bills, etc. to an elderly neighbor, relative, etc.

2507. If you see an elderly person walking slowly across a street, offer to help or at least walk with them while they cross

2508. Offer your seat to an elderly person if you see them standing in a waiting room, on a bus, etc.

2509. If you see an elderly person in the grocery store having trouble lifting something heavy or they have a question and can't find a store employee, offer to help them

2510. Practice patience at all times when talking, walking, eating, etc. with an elderly person Always show them respect and courtesy

2511. Many elderly people are alone due to a death of a spouse and/or their children live elsewhere. Offer to take them out to eat every once in a while with your family or invite them over to eat with your family. They can always say no—but will probably say yes!

2512. If you know of an elderly person with a dog, offer to walk the dog every once in a while. Make sure there is food for the animal and all their shots are up-to-date

2513. Organize or join a committee at church that provides rides to the elderly in the congregation to doctor appointments, the grocery store, etc.

2514. Visit relatives, neighbors, etc. who are in assisted living/nursing homes. Visit regularly but not always the same day/time. Make sure the staff knows you will come by at different times. Make sure everything is in order and your relative or friend is being taken care of

2515. When visiting someone in a nursing home, bring a gift for the staff—cookies, candy, flowers, etc. Let them know you appreciate their good job and that you notice what they do for your friend/relative

2516. Help fix up the nursing home room with things your friend or relative will enjoy, such as family photos made into a collage, pictures drawn by a loved child, etc.

2517. Bring magazines, large-print books, etc. to share with other residents in the nursing facility

2518. If you see another resident who has no one visiting them, stop by and say hello. Maybe bring them a little something special

2519. Talk to your elderly relative about their life and make a recording of the conversations. Transcribe them and put together a family history and give them a copy. Give a copy to your other relatives so they have a record of it, too

2520. Research your family genealogy and talk to your relatives to get more information. Find out if you are eligible for membership in certain organizations—Daughters of the American Revolution, Sons of the Republic of Texas, Daughters of Civil War Veterans. If so, submit the name of the elderly relative and frame the certificate that comes with the membership and give it to them

2521. If you notice that your friend or relative needs some clothes washed or a bathroom cleaned—do it

2522. If you notice that your friend or relative is developing signs of hoarding things, dementia, etc., don't ignore it! Call their doctor and find them some help. Things will get much worse if you don't

2523. Offer to mow the lawn, rake leaves, or spruce up the house for an elderly friend or relative

2524. If they are still driving, make sure their car is being maintained—oil changed regularly, car washed and detailed, etc. Make sure they have your telephone number to call if they break down or have a flat

2525. If you know how, offer to help your elderly friend or relative with their taxes

2526. If you are qualified, volunteer at your church or city/county community agency that helps senior citizens understand and fill out their state and federal income taxes

2527. Listen to their stories—you just might learn something

2528. If you find out someone has taken monetary advantage of your elderly relative or neighbor, help them find restitution and get it resolved. Get their clergy involved—there may be a committee of lawyers, accountants, etc. through church that volunteers to help parishioners with just these issues

2529. Offer to drive an elderly neighbor or relative to church services every week If possible, offer to take them to breakfast or lunch afterward

2530. Make sure you have the telephone number of grown children or relatives of your elderly neighbors so you can contact them in case of an emergency

2531. If your elderly neighbor or relative needs special equipment such as a cane or wheelchair, help them contact the right agency to get it

2532. If your elderly neighbor or relative is having yard work or house repairs done, politely let the vendor know that you will help keep an eye on things to make sure the job is completed to your neighbor's satisfaction

2533. When your child or other children are selling magazine subscriptions through school or church, give a subscription of a magazine on a favorite topic to an elderly friend or relative

Pie in the Sky

2534. Organize a bake sale in your neighborhood or parish to raise money for a local food bank and offer only pie—slices or whole pies—and organize it so there are plenty of people making pies. Promote it so there are plenty of people purchasing pies!

2535. When your parish has a fish fry to raise money during Lent, offer to provide the dessert and organize a group of people who will make pies to sell by the slice to donate back to the fish-fry fundraiser

2536. Join or organize a committee of parents from the parish school to bake pies. Deliver them to families who have a child just starting kindergarten or who are new to the school. It is a great way to meet the parents of the new students and to make them feel part of the school family

2537. Organize a pie-throwing contest to raise money for your favorite charity. The throwers could be divided into men, women, and children. Give a prize pie for the longest throws!

2538. Organize a pie-eating contest to raise money for your favorite charity

2539. Organize a pie-judging contest and charge an entry fee. Give a monetary prize for the winners in different categories such as best fruit pie, best cream pie, etc. Donate the profits to your favorite charity

2540. Organize a pie-tasting party to raise money for a favorite charity. Invite people over to taste pies and then to donate what they think a pie is worth to take the rest of it home. Many times people will donate more than what you asked for—especially for charity

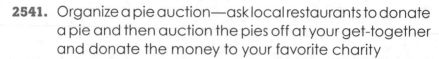

2541. Organize a pie auction—ask local restaurants to donate a pie and then auction the pies off at your get-together and donate the money to your favorite charity

2542. Organize an art contest at school with pie as the subject. Charge a small fee for the children to enter—$1 or so—and display the entries at school. Ask teachers to anonymously judge the entries, and give the winners a pie for a prize. Donate the money back to the school

2543. Organize parents during Teacher Appreciation Week at school to make a pie for each teacher and give to them with a note thanking them for a job well done

2544. Organize a writing contest at school with pie as the theme—short story, poem, etc. Charge a small entry fee—$1 or so—for every entry. Ask teachers to judge the entries and give a pie to the winners of each category

2545. When your children have friends over to spend the night, get them away from the television and bake a pie together! Show them how to use a rolling pin and/or whip egg whites into peaks, etc.

2546. Volunteer to make pies for your child's math teacher to use in demonstrating graphs—and then the children can each have a piece!

2547. Don't forget that pizza is a pie—let your children invite their friends over and have a pizza pie making party and teach them how to make the dough, they can pick their favorite toppings, help them bake it and then everyone can enjoy!

Break the Addiction

2548. Recognize and realize when you have a bad habit that needs to be broken. Ask for help—there are many self/help books/organizations/doctors/clergy, etc. available to help you

2549. Do not let a bad habit/addiction/illegal activities take over your life, ruin a marriage, ruin you relationships, or hurt yourself or anyone else

2550. Do not protect other people who are hurting themselves or others through their addictions/habits. Do not tolerate drug/alcohol use and abuse by your friends

2551. Plan an intervention to help a friend or family member confront a problem can be very difficult. There are books that explain how to do this and there are organizations/health care professionals who can help

2552. Don't allow yourself to condone a behavior that is destructive in others Don't be codependent or an enabler—talk to other friends, family, clergy, doctors, and read on what you can do to help the other person

2553. If they won't let you help them—leave knowing you did everything you could and you have no regrets

Weddings/Divorces/Funerals

2554. If you are able and are a close family friend of the bride or groom or a member of the groom's family, volunteer to host a bridal shower for the bride

2555. Great game for showers: Have everyone fill out a recipe card and give it to the bride with a recipe box and she'll have a stack of family recipes as a priceless gift

2556. Get together with other family members and ask everyone to finish a quilt square (you can have a theme or not) and make a quilt out of it and give it as a gift to the bride and groom

2557. If guests will be traveling to attend the wedding, offer your guest room

2558. Offer to pick up guests at airports and train stations

2559. Get together with other family members and make crafty holiday decorations for the couple-to-be—napkin rings and holders for 4th of July, Halloween decorations, Christmas tree ornaments, Valentine's Day wreath, etc. and give to the happy couple

2560. If there is a divorce in the family, try not to take sides

2561. Don't let divorce stop you from taking your grandchildren fishing

2562. Plan time together with your grandchildren regularly after divorce

2563. Divorce can be complicated if one or both of the people in the marriage has had an affair. If that other person is now going to be part of your family, try to remain neutral unless you feel very strongly about what happened

2564. Divorce is a especially difficult on the children involved Let them know you love them no matter what and this is not their fault. Let them know you are always there for them and you won't talk bad about either one of their parents

2565. Funerals bring family together like a wedding or a party—but with no joy. Don't forget to have parties, reunions, or something joyful that brings these people together occasionally

2566. If there is death in the family or friendship, don't wait—call, write, contact the widow, widower, survivors immediately and offer to do whatever you can to help

2567. The energy and endless tasks before a funeral end and then the survivors are left with a lot of time and sadness a week or two after the funeral. Don't forget about them—send them letters, emails, call them, offer to take them out—whatever you can do. They need you and your attention long after the wake and funeral are over

2568. If there was a cause or charity that the deceased felt strongly about, donate to that charity and ask that a thank you be sent to the family

2569. In the event of a death in the neighborhood, offer up your guest room for traveling family and friends

2570. Offer to cook and serve for the funeral dinner

Come Join Our Family

2571. If you are going to welcome a pet into your family, make sure you are prepared to take care of this pet for the rest of its life

2572. If you and your family are able to—consider becoming a foster parent. Consider taking siblings, if you can

2573. If your in-laws adopt a child, welcome this new child into the family with no reservations. Always consider them part of the family

2574. Welcoming new in-laws can be very joyous or very stressful. If your child has become engaged, make sure your child knows you love their prospective spouse and you want them to be happy. They are grown-ups and will make their own decisions—it's up to you to be welcoming to the new family member

2575. Children of divorce often face new challenges—such as fending for themselves when their mother has to go back to work. Make an effort to help the children if you can—if you are a neighbor, watch out for them, let them know they can call you if they need anything, etc.

2576. Don't forget the neighbor who is a widow or alone. Invite them over to eat or for a cup of coffee. Offer to drive them somewhere if they need to go

2577. Offer to throw a baby shower for a family member who is having a baby, or a bridal shower for someone in the family who is going to get married

2578. It can be a difficult situation if your parent, who might have been a widow or widower for some time, remarries Be nice to this new person who is making your mother or father so happy

2579. It can be a terrible situation if your spouse leaves you for another person, especially if you have children who will be visiting and spending time with them. Try to remain neutral and refrain from criticizing the new spouse.

2580. If you are able, "adopt" a child through a mission or sponsorship through your church or a reputable agency You can send them money, toys, clothing, etc. and you get an update on how they are doing

2581. Work with your employer to develop adoption benefits

If I Had A Hammer

2582. Volunteer to work with Habitat for Humanity and help build houses for people who can't afford to do it themselves

2583. Volunteer to help through the St. Vincent de Paul Society in your area to do minor repairs for the families who are in need—fix broken appliances or patch holes that the families cannot afford to pay someone else to do

2584. Volunteer to help at church or school when they need volunteers to help with various projects—doing maintenance work, building a stage for a school pageant, building a manger scene during Advent, etc.

2585. With your children, hand make a crèche and give it to your pastor at church or your child's youth leader

2586. Volunteer to help families at church or school who need work done because someone in the family is disabled—such as building a ramp, installing a "grab bar" in the bathroom, lowering cabinets, etc.

2587. If you are good with cars, volunteer through church to help parishioners who are having a difficult financial time or who are elderly and need car repairs

2588. If you work in a trade—plumbing, electrical, carpentry, etc.—volunteer your expertise at church to help needy families in the parish with repairs

2589. Volunteer your expertise to help the organization with repairs and upkeep of its own facilities

2590. After a storm, offer to help people clear branches, brush, etc. from their property. Having a chain saw is a real help, as is having a pick-up truck or some type of vehicle in which you can haul away debris

2591. Have fun with your children and help them build a tree house or playhouse

2592. Be willing to teach friends, family, and neighbors basic mechanical and home maintenance skills

2593. Help your new neighbors paint—and get acquainted along the way

2594. Help upgrade, repair, or tear down eye-sores in the neighborhood

2595. Organize a repair day for seniors and veterans. Get a group together to paint, repair and clean-up for those that may not have the ability

2596. Build a dog house

2597. Build your own home

2598. Join a barn raising

2599. Build a family heirloom (table, chair, chest, etc.)

2600. Teach someone else about woodworking

2601. Learn to lay bricks

2602. Work on community infrastructure projects

2603. Hang pictures for someone moving into a new place

2604. Decorate outdoor spaces for the holidays

2605. Build a picnic table for the community center

2606. Build a bird or bat house

2607. Refurbish your mother's favorite piece of furniture

2608. Put in a sitting bench in your front yard for people who need a place to sit and watch the world go by

2609. Work with a group to install new playground equipment

2610. Create a balance beam for your kids to practice

2611. Build a deck for parties

2612. Make a wooden instrument

2613. Whittle

2614. Teach someone else to whittle

2615. Make a rocking chair for someone's front porch

Care and Feeding of Friends

2616. Give a rose bush, hydrangea, peony, or other living plant instead of "funeral flowers" in memory of a friend or relative

2617. Make a "road trip" with your friends, even if it is just an overnight get-together for dinner, a movie, and quality "talking" time

2618. Send get well cards, but don't stop at just one if the person will have a long recovery—send one every two weeks (put it on your calendar as a reminder)

2619. Fix a meal for new parents, a family grieving the death of a loved one, a new neighbor, or the family of someone going through medical treatments. Chicken Tetrazzini, salad fixings (bag of lettuce, croutons, and dressing), a loaf of French bread, and a cake is an easy meal. This is always appreciated, and it's also good for you

2620. Start a "nothing NEW for a year" challenge with friends—everyone saves

2621. Introduce your friends to other friends they might not know

2622. Set a date to eat lunch with a good friend every month, without fail

2623. Order a step counter or two as gifts for friends and family

2624. Buy inexpensive packets of flower and vegetable seeds and give to friends, neighbors, and family. This is a great way to introduce and encourage gardening

2625. Start a healthy-recipe exchange with a group of friends

2626. Interview your friends on video camera, edit and give them their personal documentary

2627. Share your plants (flower and vegetable) or "cuttings" of your plants with family and friends. Once plants are established, they are easy to transplant

2628. When friends are unemployed, present them with a "job search survival kit"

2629. Help out of work friends network on the internet

2630. Brainstorm new ideas with friends

2631. Brainstorm solutions to your problems and theirs

2632. Set up blind dates for single friends

2633. Present access passes to the art museum

2634. Teach a friend to cook

2635. Have a wine tasting party with all your friends

2636. Always have a sympathetic ear

2637. Don't try to solve a friend's problem, walking with them to a solution

2638. Focus on what friends feel right now

2639. Respect privacy

2640. Make a point of remember friends that have passed

2641. Encourage a friend in their latest hair-brain idea

2642. Don't play mommy or daddy in a friendship

2643. Be honest

2644. Don't set a relationship status—like all things, friendships evolve

2645. Link your social profile to theirs

2646. Avoid being judgmental

2647. Don't keep score

2648. Notice the little stuff

2649. Choose friendships wisely

2650. Be responsible with what your friends trust to you

2651. Don't be afraid to stand up to themselves

2652. Check on them during a crisis

2653. Don't ditch a friend for a date

2654. Trust a friend with your secrets

2655. Don't use pressure to force a friend to do something they do not want to do

2656. Have good times

Not in English

2657. Support Catholic Charities and their refugee program

2658. Start an English as a second language program

2659. Act as interpreter when dealing with their children's schools and official services

2660. Make an effort to introduce yourself to a new immigrant and ask if they need help. Be a friend to their children

2661. If there are immigrants coming into your parish, offer to start a committee to welcome them

2662. Ask for volunteers from the parish who speak different languages to be "on call" when needed

2663. Talk to the pastor about purchasing sacramental preparation materials and other items in different languages

2664. Volunteer through a nonprofit agency to help immigrants in your community find jobs, find housing, get a driver's license, etc. Remember—your ancestors immigrated to this country, too!

2665. Practice Christianity toward people who come to the United States to make a better life for themselves and their families. Do not disparage them, make life difficult for them, or tolerate racist remarks from others

2666. Learn another language

2667. Tutor would-be citizens for their tests

2668. Respect cultural differences

Write a Letter

2669. Write a thank you note for every gift you receive

2670. Make a commitment to write at least one thank you note a week to a coworker who has performed above and beyond the regular duties

2671. Write a nice little note to someone and put it on their car windshield or driver's side window. They will be very pleasantly surprised when they leave at the end of the day and see a nice note from you!

2672. Write a thank you note to someone you normally wouldn't—to your letter carrier, the newspaper delivery person, the trash hauler, etc.

2673. Write a letter to the management of a business complimenting a salesperson or employee who really did an outstanding job

2674. Write a letter to your children and put it in your safe deposit box for them to find when they find your will

2675. Write a love letter to your spouse

2676. Write a letter with each Christmas card you sent—a personal letter to the recipient

2677. Get involved and write a letter to your local state representative or federal legislator about an issue that is important to you

2678. Before you tell someone off or say something you wish you hadn't—write it down in a letter, set it aside for a while, and then come back to it. You'll be able to look at it through calmer eyes, and you'll probably be very glad you waited to express your rage!

Money Matters

2679. Turn off the television—you'll have less exposure to guilt-inducing ads, plus it saves electricity

2680. Master the 30-day rule—wait 30 days before buying, then ask yourself if you still want it

2681. Call your credit card company and ask for a rate reduction (the worst they can say is "no")

2682. Switch your bank accounts to a bank that pays interest on check, as well as savings, doesn't charge for online bill paying, and has low maintenance fees

2683. Give up expensive habits—you know the ones—alcohol, cigarettes, and drugs

2684. Cook for yourself—cut back on convenience foods (fast food, microwavable meals, etc.)

2685. Drink more water

2686. Turn off the lights when you leave a room

2687. Turn off the front porch light when you go to bed

2688. Install a programmable thermostat

2689. Use LED or CFL light bulbs, instead of traditional incandescent bulbs

2690. Make a quadruple batch of a casserole and freeze it in convenient sizes for later use

2691. Invest in a freezer

2692. Look for a cheaper place to live

2693. Sign up for every free customer rewards program at all the stores you shop

2694. "Make" the holidays and birthdays bright with home-made gifts

2695. Clean out your closet, basement, garage—and have a yard sale

2696. Invite friends over instead of going out

2697. Write out a shopping list before going shopping and don't go shopping when you are hungry

2698. Shop yard sales

2699. Buy new appliances based on reliability and energy rating, instead of on price

2700. Hide your credit cards—better yet, freeze them in a block of ice

2701. Air up your tires to their proper weight

2702. Clean or replace car air filters

2703. Keep up on home and auto maintenance—it saves on bigger repairs later

2704. Swap media entertainment (DVDs, CDs) with friends and neighbors instead of buying more

2705. Take public transportation

2706. Carpool and ride share

2707. Pack your own food for a road trip instead of stopping at restaurants

2708. Use the Library for new entertainment

2709. Cut your own hair

2710. Check your cell phone program for services you don't use and cancel them

2711. Get a crock pot

2712. Check out free community events

2713. Consolidate debt

2714. Check out ALL the benefits offered by your employer

2715. Watch the speed limit—tickets cost money, speeding eats gas and is unsafe

2716. Consider buying a late model car versus brand new one

2717. Watch your entertainment dollars when out with friends—encourage them to go a little "cheaper"

2718. Don't go all out when entertaining children—kids just want to have fun

2719. Shop for clothes that will stay in fashion longer—go for the classics

2720. Instead of discarding clothing that has been torn—repair it

2721. Don't spend money to feel better about yourself and relieve stress

2722. Talk to loved ones about your dreams—saving for dreams makes the task easier

2723. Wash your hands—less colds and flu—less medical expenses

2724. Buy generic

2725. Brown bag it at the job at least 4 times a week

2726. Instead of giving things for birthdays and holidays— give your time and service (make your own gift card and present it)

2727. Check out the sales at the grocery store before shopping—plan your purchases and meals around sales and seasons

2728. Price compare seriously—is another grocery store cheaper? Can I get the same item somewhere else for less?

2729. Switch to term life insurance

2730. Buy only the insurance you need in your life, without the bells-and-whistles you don't need

2731. Master the 10-second rule: whenever you pick up an item to go in the cart that was not on your shopping list, think about it for 10 seconds before buying

2732. Eat breakfast—it gives you energy and helps the mid-morning cravings for junk food

2733. Swap services with your neighbors—babysitting for car repair, yard work for window cleaning, etc.

2734. Embrace leftovers

2735. Get rid of club memberships and subscriptions that you do not use

2736. Do not go to stores and shopping centers for entertainment

2737. If something is broken, give do-it-yourself repair a try

2738. Check out programs with your parks and recreations department for exercise

2739. Always ask that fees be waived

2740. Eat less meat

2741. Start a garden

2742. Do an energy check on your home for heat loss, energy use, and moisture damage

2743. Make your own wine or beer

2744. Exchange coupons with a friend or neighbor instead of pitching the ones you won't use

2745. Make sure you use a surge protector for electrical devices and turn the power OFF when not in use

2746. Cancel cable and satellite services you don't use regularly

2747. Pay bills online (saves postage)

2748. Plan vacations that you can afford—go camping, visit friends, take day or weekend trips instead of a bigger trip

2749. Buy staples such as toilet paper in bulk

2750. Don't beat yourself up for mistakes—stay positive

2751. Save your change in a jar all year long and at the end of the year roll the coins with your family, take it to the bank and get cash, and donate the money to your favorite charity

2752. If you usually eat lunch or supper out several times a week, eat at home or bring a lunch more often. Put $5 a week in a jar (the $5 you would have spent on the one meal you didn't buy out) and at the end of the year, donate that money to your favorite charity

2753. Make a family budget and stick to it

2754. Give stocks to your favorite charity—you won't pay capital gains tax, and the current value is tax deductible

2755. Make a retirement plan for yourself and your spouse. Include plans that will allow one of you to survive, in the event of death of the other

2756. Make "humane" investments—know where your money is going and the type of company you are investing in

2757. Keep insurance policy coverage up-to-date with today's standards

2758. Drop the paid TV services

2759. Reduce phone extras such as call forwarding or call waiting

2760. Cancel your land line in favor of cell service (or vice versa)

2761. Seek a cheaper long distance carrier or switch to Internet calling if you have high-speed service

2762. Investigate whether bundled service (phone, high-speed Internet and cable television) might save you money

2763. Wash only full loads of dishes or clothes

2764. Use a clothesline and use your dryer just to soften air-dried clothes

2765. Use shades, blinds and drapes to regulate your home temperature. Keep them open in the winter to let in light and drawn in the summer to block the sun's rays

2766. Wear a sweater in winter and shorts in the summer so you're not overheating or cooling your house

2767. Switch to compact-fluorescent bulbs, and turn them off when not needed. Turn off TVs, computers and other electronics when not in use

2768. Keep a "nest egg" for emergencies

2769. Plan for your children's education when they are born

2770. Consider investing as a family. Make sure you have a family corporation in place to do it

2771. Buying used cars and driving them for years is a great way to reduce your lifetime transportation expenditures.

2772. Raise the deductibles on your auto-insurance policy

2773. Get all the discounts you deserve on your insurance, such as good-driver, good-student and multiple-car discounts

2774. If you're driving less, tell your insurer; you may get a cheaper rate

2775. Cancel collision and comprehensive insurance on cars older than five to seven years

2776. Investigate carpools and public transportation. Cities often have online trip planners to help you figure out the system. See if your employer offers any subsidies

2777. Avoid repair bills by maintaining your vehicles properly with regular oil and filter changes

2778. Group your errands and, if you have more than one car, use the vehicle with better gas mileage

2779. Bring lunches and snacks to work

2780. Cook once, eat twice. Double whatever you're making and freeze the excess for a later meal

2781. Make at least one or two meatless meals each week

2782. Avoid over-packaged, over-processed and highly advertised foods The closer a food is to its natural state, the less it tends to cost

2783. Buy fruits and vegetables in season. Also check out your local farmer's market

2784. Cruise through your fridge daily to use items before they go bad

2785. Give up a food vice (chocolate, soda, snack foods)

2786. Use the weekly grocery store circulars to see what's on sale and plan meals accordingly

2787. Inventory your wardrobe and buy pieces that work with what you already own

2788. Avoid dry-clean-only clothing

2789. Purchase a product that lets you "dry clean" in your dryer

2790. Make hair appointments at beauty schools rather than full-priced salons

2791. Drop your health club and form a walking or jogging group with friends

2792. Hold a clothing swap with friends

2793. Ask friends and relatives for hand-me-downs

2794. Give kids a clothing allowance or offer "matching funds" for what they want to buy

2795. Check out consignment and thrift stores for lightly used items

2796. Don't cut back on your 401K or IRA contributions, unless you have no choice, and do not cash them in or borrow against them, unless you have not other choice

Remembering Those in Prison

2797. Buy and send a bunch of books to a prison in your community for its library.

2798. Send some new faith-inspiring books in care of the prison chaplain

2799. Organize a Mother's or Father's Day visit to a prison— charter a bus with chaperones to bring children to visit their parent in prison

2800. Donate to support anti-gang programs in prison

2801. Volunteer to be an in-prison tutor

2802. Work with ex-cons on interview skills, job applications and resumes

2803. Hire an ex-con or someone on probation

2804. Donate to support addiction treatment and prevention programs

2805. Become a prison fellowship volunteer

2806. Volunteer to teach job skills to ex-cons

2807. Become a pen pal with an inmate

2808. Join and support ministry at a prison close to you

2809. Research support groups for ex-cons. Volunteer time to the cause

2810. Volunteer to assist ex-cons with tax filings

2811. Become a prison mentor

Rock Bottom

2812. Practice being appreciative and thankful even when you don't feel appreciative or thankful

2813. Trust more deeply

2814. See yourself as God sees you

2815. Write notes of appreciation to three people who have made a difference in your life and send them in the mail

2816. Watch a comedy movie with a friend– laughter is a great medicine

2817. Visit an animal shelter and experience unconditional love of animals. Consider taking one home

2818. Spend as much time as you can with people who are cheerful and optimistic

2819. Take a brisk walk outside

2820. Write in your journal

2821. Try to spend at least an hour every day doing something that you enjoy

2822. Resist temptation

2823. Let yourself go occasionally If you feel tense or uptight. Go outside and smash a tennis ball or football or dig in the garden!

2824. Don't be afraid to cry. Tears shed for emotional reasons contain special proteins—crying is a useful and constructive way of dealing with sadness. Crying will make you feel rested, calmer and happier

2825. Talk to your friends. Explain to them how you feel. If they are real friends they will want to listen—and want to help you. If you don't have any friends, ring the Samaritans—the telephone number will be in the phone book

2826. Go fishing

2827. Help an elder of your family, and listen to their thoughts—they've seem more of life than you

2828. Learn to play again

2829. Face the fears that are holding you back head-on

2830. Take up a new hobby—maybe something that you've always wanted to try. Donate the rewards of the hobby

2831. Clean someone else's house, and make their day

2832. Fill up your schedule with activities that make you feel good and do good for others

2833. Help a friend with writing, printing, and submitting resumes and cover letters is seek a job

2834. Help a friend research new career options

2835. Search for new career options yourself

2836. Get a makeover

2837. Get a massage

2838. See a doctor if the depression continues

2839. Discover your purpose

2840. Get out in the sun—Vitamin D is very good for mood

2841. Take a serious look at what (and possibly who) is causing these feelings. Make the changes you need to make

2842. Give up what should have been for what is and what can be

2843. Send a get-well card to yourself. Write in it 3 accomplishments you have made in the last six months—bask in the glory

2844. Pray

2845. Volunteer to be a "bell-ringer" for Salvation Army

2846. Serve food at a soup kitchen

2847. Eat only healthy, organic food for two weeks

2848. Exercise (swimming is great)

2849. Throw pennies in a wishing well

2850. Force yourself to smile—it really helps

2851. Be open to any outcome—life changes moment by moment

2852. Break free of judging other people and yourself

2853. Forgive others

2854. Forgive yourself

FreeCycle

2855. Leave your unused coupons in the grocery store right by the product in the store. The coupon was free to you—you didn't use it, but someone else will surely benefit

2856. Instead of throwing away useful household items, advertising them as "free" on Internet bulletin boards, such as craigslist.com

2857. Start a kids' clothes sharing circle with mothers of other young children

2858. Barter your services. A neighbor might need help with a household repair that you know how to do, in exchange, that neighbor can babysit for you for free

2859. Start a Neighborhood Watch Security for all and expense to no one

2860. Join a freecycle meet-up group—go to http://freecycle.meetup.com

2861. Organize a Swap-a-Rama. Each attendee must bring a minimum of one garment in good condition, to exchange with someone else. Set up sewing machines and craft benches so alternations can be made. Then hold a Swap-a-Rama fashion show at the end of the day

2862. Go dumpster diving

2863. Collect and use your coupons

2864. Check out free entertainment—free days at the zoo, etc.

2865. Start a neighborhood DVD lending library

2866. Start a neighborhood "night at the movies." Project the movie on to a flat garage door or side of a house (maybe someone has an old projector screen) and invite everyone to BYOB and BYOF

Free Fun Weekend

2867. Check out the community calendar for free activities around down

2868. Visit your community library

2869. Get involved in community sports

2870. Get your financial papers in order

2871. Check out some podcasts

2872. Play board games

2873. Learn how to juggle

2874. Teach yourself how to change the oil in your car

2875. Meet your neighbors

2876. Have a "cupboard potluck"

2877. Clean out your media collection—books, DVDs, CDs, old vinyl albums

2878. Make a 101 Goals in 1001 Days list

2879. Make decisions about and write out your will (www. doyourownwill.com)

2880. Do a household maintenance walkthrough

2881. Organize a walking tour

2882. Teach yourself how to knit (www.learntoknit.com)

2883. Take some digital photographs

2884. Share those digital photographs with others

2885. Start a blog on a topic that interests you

2886. Organize a potluck block party

2887. Visit a free museum or zoo (many have "free" days)

2888. Learn the basics of a new topic. Go to MIT's Open Course Ware (http://ocwmit.edu/OcwWeb/web/home/home/index.htm)

2889. Cook some meals in advance

2890. Build a basic net worth calculator for yourself (http://www.msnbc.msn.com/id/9745956

2891. Hold a quilting bee

2892. Try out some great open source and free software

2893. Practice origami

2894. Make a how-to video for You Tube

2895. Do a bill reduction plan

2896. Play football/soccer

2897. Scan your old photographs

2898. Have a film festival with your old DVDs

2899. Seduce your spouse

2900. Do some professional networking

2901. Practice yoga—or try it for the first time

2902. Cut you own hair

2903. Do a neighborhood clean-up

2904. Build some paper airplanes, and teach someone else how

2905. Rearrange the furniture

2906. Read an entertaining book

2907. Build a giant blanket fort

2908. Call a family member or friend you haven't spoken to for a while

2909. Start on observation notebook on a nature walk

2910. Start a compost bin

2911. Have a yard sale

2912. Learn a foreign language

2913. Deep clean the room in the house you spend the most time in

2914. Make some homemade greeting and holiday cards

2915. Take a nap

2916. Dig up your family free (www.genealogy.com)

2917. Sit down with your spouse for an afternoon and just talk

2918. Do some puzzles

2919. Volunteer your time

2920. Turn on the water sprinkler, and run through it like a kid

2921. Try a basic meditation technique

2922. Get involved in an open source programming project

2923. Teach yourself a card trick

2924. Attend a religious service

2925. Start a workout routine

2926. Read a "great" book

2927. Go swimming

2928. Acquire a pen pal and faithfully correspond

2929. Get involved with public access television

2930. Blow bubbles

2931. Start a journal

2932. Write a letter to your future children or grandchildren

2933. Make Christmas gifts in advance

2934. Go "coupon scavenging"

2935. Pickup a musical instrument and learn it

2936. Plan next year's summer vacation

2937. Pick up (and read) a copy of the town's free newspaper

2938. Play with a pet—even if it is someone else's

2939. Go on a wandering walk

2940. Exchange massages with your spouse

2941. Help out an elderly or disabled friend or neighbor

2942. Start a book club, or join one

2943. Play a card game

2944. Have an "entertainment swap with a friend—exchange DVDs, CDs, etc. with each other

2945. Take a child to a playground and actually play with them

2946. Explore a blog you like

2947. Work for a political campaign

2948. Clean out a closet

2949. Play Frisbee in the park

2950. Take a long, soaking bath

2951. Visit the magazine room at the library

2952. Attend a dress rehearsal of a community theater group— it's usually free

2953. Attend a free community class or lecture

2954. Donate some unwanted things to charity

2955. Volunteer to be a Salvation Army bell ringer

2956. Discover new music that you like

2957. Build a cardboard castle

2958. Do some amateur stargazing

2959. Take a stab at writing poetry or haiku

2960. Go for a bike ride

Kitchen Rescue

2961. Don't fear the crock pot

2962. You can almost never over-season a dish

2963. Hone your knives

2964. Use fresh ingredients

2965. Always make stock out of leftover bones and leftover vegetables

2966. De-glaze at every opportunity

2967. Stick with comfort foods at first when learning to cook

2968. Try cooking something familiar without a recipe

2969. Get others involved—friends cook with friends

For Whom the Bell Tolls

2970. Read John Donne's *No Man is an Island*

2971. Have a Mass said for the deceased members of your family

2972. With older-age children visit the cemetery where family is buried and share stories of what they did and how they lived

2973. See that you have an up-to-date will

2974. Plan your funeral, choosing songs, readings, and so forth

2975. Clean out your closets once a year

Once In a Lifetime

2976. These are things that you will do only once, but would be an experience of a lifetime

2977. Take a hot air balloon ride in the early evening

2978. Take a helicopter ride

2979. Feel the freedom of skydiving—once—don't tempt fate a second time!

2980. Take a drive across the county—do not drive on interstates and do not eat at fast food restaurants

2981. Write and file your will. Be sure to leave 10% to your church—you may have had a hard time tithing while you were alive, but be sure to tithe in your estate!

2982. Rent a movie theatre. As a surprise, bring your wife out to the movies, but instead of watching the movie you said you would see, watch your own wedding on the big screen

2983. Run a marathon—or at least walk it—just finish!

2984. Take your kids and your grandkids on a special vacation—all on you! Be aware of children's schedules

2985. Write a movie script, and donate all the earnings

2986. Read *2001 Things to Do Before You Die*

2987. Read *1000 Places to Visit Before You Die*

2988. Organize a plan to build a new community center

2989. Run for public office, and keep your campaign promises

2990. Hunt up an old boyfriend/girlfriend and thank them for the time you spent together

2991. Make a religious pilgrimage to Mecca, Santiago de Compostela, and Jerusalem

2992. Light a candle in the Holocaust Memorial Museum's Hall of Remembrance

2993. Write every family member and friend and tell them what you appreciate about them

2994. Send your parents, or older aunts and uncles on a cruise or a safari

2995. Help clear old mine fields in the Middle East

2996. Take the summer off to organize free health clinics in rural areas

2997. Give a $100 bottle of wine to each of your closest friends

2998. Pay for a stranger's college education

2999. Give new computers to six Senior Centers, and pay for the internet connection

3000. Finance libraries in five small towns

3001. Form your own charity foundation for a cause near and dear to your heart

3002. Spend one month completely alone

3003. Pay for a disabled veteran's rent for a year

3004. Make a pilgrimage to your family's home country

3005. Give ten people $100 to invest, with a goal of making $100,000 for charity

3006. Help rebuild New Orleans

3007. Explore Paris catacombs

3008. Go to Stonehenge on the winter solstice

3009. Take a pilgrimage to Angkor Wat

3010. Ski in a shopping center in Dubai

3011. Compete on a game show

3012. Go on an archaeological dig

3013. Leave the world in a better place than you found it

3014. When traveling to Europe, spend some time at a monastery or convent guest house. (See Liguori Publications' *Europe's Monastery and Convent Guest Houses*.) You will be asked to pray the Liturgy of the Hours and assist at Mass with the community

3015. Take a year's sabbatical and donate that time to a worthy mission

Satisfying Basic Needs for the Homeless

3016. Donate complimentary shampoo, soaps, etc. from hotels to the homeless

3017. Help cook dinner for the homeless at the shelter

3018. Organize a food drive through your church, social group, or friends and donate to a homeless feeding program

3019. Employ a homeless person at a livable wage, not just minimum wage

3020. Donate diapers and wipes to homeless shelters

3021. Volunteer to tutor a homeless child through your local school district

3022. Donate your furniture to a social program providing housing for the homeless. Contact your local social services

3023. Buy extra school supplies and donate them to homeless students

3024. Become informed and be an advocate for community solutions

3025. Volunteer to assist homeless teens with Stand Up for Kids

3026. Donate good quality work-appropriate clothing to women's shelters and homeless shelters

3027. Respond with a kind word when you are approached for a handout for coffee or a meal

3028. Put your professional talents to work as a volunteer for re-education and change

3029. Donate sleeping bags to the homeless

3030. Mentor a homeless family through a shelter

3031. Donate spare sporting events tickets to an agency supporting the homeless

3032. Make sack lunches and give out at the beginning of the day at a shelter

3033. Volunteer at a day care center for homeless parents

3034. Carry fast food gift cards to give to the homeless who are hungry

3035. Conduct a kitchenware drive at your workplace to help with new housing for homeless women

3036. Volunteer with Habitat for Humanity to help with construction of housing for low-income families

3037. Donate new reading glasses through shelters

3038. Adopt an agency that serves the homeless and give them year-round support

3039. Donate new socks, underwear, jeans, work boots, sneakers and t-shirts to the homeless shelter

3040. Donate children's reading books to educational programs and women's shelters

3041. Ask your school what they need for the poor children and provide it

3042. Volunteer to staff the "thrift store" at a shelter

3043. Make welcome kits with everyday household basics for the homeless in transition and donate to the Salvation Army

3044. Educate your children to respect the dignity of all human beings

3045. Get Your house of worship involved with the shelter system

3046. Organize a fund raiser for your favorite charity serving the homeless

3047. Volunteer legal services, management services, clerical services to any agency helping the homeless

3048. Donate picture magazines to agency waiting rooms

3049. Adopt a family for the holidays through the Salvation Army

3050. Prepare "birthday baskets" for homeless children. Include cake mix, frosting, candles, birthday napkins, favors, a gift, etc. to be used at shelters

3051. Serve on the board of directors of one of the agencies serving the homeless and assist with decision-making that helps the homeless

3052. Volunteer income tax filing assistance at any agency that helps the homeless

3053. Recognize a friend's birthday by making donations in their names to a women's shelter

3054. Write to elected officials and ask them what they are doing to help the homeless and discourage them from tearing down low-income housing

3055. Ask a homeless shelter or women's shelter what they need and provide it

3056. Encourage your mayor and commissioners to build affordable housing

3057. Share this list with work associates, family and friends

Advocate for the Homeless

3058. Know the issues

3059. Connect with a local coalition

3060. Network with advocates in other cities

3061. Engage your local elected officials

3062. Personally meet with your legislator

3063. Involve the media

3064. Get involved with a local street newspaper

3065. Register the homeless to vote, and then help them on election day

3066. Encourage advocacy where it counts

3067. Start a blog on the issue

3068. Create an online group talking about the issues

3069. Organize action groups

3070. Campaign for politicians that share your views on the issue

3071. Set up information booths at craft fairs and street fairs

Fight Poverty

3072. Eat meatless meals 2 times a week

3073. Find a gripping picture or video having to do with poverty and publish it on the web

3074. Organize a Hunger 101 class for a local youth group

3075. Make a personal fund-raising page on Firstgiving.com

3076. Make a loan through KIVA (www.kiva.org)

3077. Sponsor job skills training in your community

3078. Recognize our shared humanity

3079. Pray for comfort and safety for the world's poor

3080. Educate yourself on the causes of poverty

3081. Join a campaign to end poverty

3082. Set up a donation fund through your payroll account

3083. Support Gulf Coast recovery

3084. Join boycotts and support unions on companies that exploit workers and prey on low-income communities

3085. Volunteer to teach English through your church or local continuing education program

3086. Take legislative action, initiate petitions for low-income housing

3087. Volunteer to babysit for a single parent after school

3088. Volunteer at a food pantry or soup kitchen

3089. Donate clothes and coats to homeless shelters and battered women's shelters

3090. Buy free trade

3091. Talk with your children about poverty

3092. Adopt a family in need for the holidays

3093. Contribute one day's salary to a food pantry

3094. Take your children to the toy store and have them pick out their favorite toys, then have them donate them to kids in need

3095. Educate yourself on your school board's stance on under programs for poor children

3096. Donate to Salvation Army

3097. Sponsor a single parent for vocational training

3098. Hold a chili cooking contest with entry fees—all money and chili going to a local soup kitchen

3099. Talk to local restaurants and grocery stores about donating leftover food at the end of the day to a soup kitchen or homeless shelter

3100. Sponsor a child in need for a full year of school—clothes, school supplies, transportation, fees, and lunch money

3101. Volunteer at shelters to help fill out applications for assistance, education, and other programs

3102. Start a literacy program at your church

3103. Offer your own home to a battered woman or crime victim

3104. Become an advocate for victims of crime

3105. Donate to international aid programs

3106. Organize a quilt raffle (or any other kind of raffle) with proceeds going to buy grocery shopping gift cards for poor families

3107. Provide daily transportation to and from work for a working poor person

3108. Take underprivileged children to an entertainment event

3109. Adopt a shelter—create a list of needed items, post at your job and collect items for donation

3110. Hire someone in need of a job

3111. Form a housing transition group—helping those moving into apartments

3112. Donate rent money to a single parent for a year

3113. Start a Junior Achievement program for poor children— they will earn money and learn about business

3114. Work with underprivileged teens to find part-time and summer jobs

3115. Teach money skills at a homeless shelter

3116. Support family farmers

3117. Provide parent support and training for the poor

3118. Create a free or low-cost day care for working poor

3119. Join Peace Corps or AmeriCorps

3120. Support companies with "fight poverty" initiatives

Build Social Capital

3121. Organize a social gathering to welcome a new neighbor

3122. Attend town meetings

3123. Support local merchants

3124. Start a front-yard/community garden

3125. Mentor someone of a different ethnic or religious group

3126. Surprise a new neighbor by making a favorite dinner—and include the recipe

3127. Plan a vacation with friends or family

3128. Help fix someone's flat tire

3129. Organize or participate in a sports league

3130. Join a gardening club

3131. Attend home parties when invited

3132. Become an organ donor or blood marrow donor

3133. Attend your children's athletic contests, plays and recitals

3134. Get to know your children's teachers

3135. Join the local Elks, Kiwanis, or Knights of Columbus

3136. Get involved with Brownies or Cub/Boy/Girl Scouts

3137. Start a monthly tea group

3138. Speak at or host a monthly brown bag lunch series at your local library

3139. Sing in a choir

3140. Get to know the clerks and salespeople at your local stores

3141. Attend PTA meetings

3142. Audition for community theater or volunteer to usher

3143. Give your park a weatherproof chess/checkers board

3144. Play cards with friends or neighbors

3145. Give to your local food bank

3146. Walk or bike to support a cause and meet others

3147. Employers: encourage volunteer/community groups to hold meetings on your site

3148. Volunteer in your child's classroom or chaperone a field trip

3149. Join or start a babysitting cooperative

3150. Attend school plays

3151. Answer surveys when asked

3152. Businesses: invite local government officials to speak at your workplace

3153. Attend Memorial Day parades and express appreciation for others

3154. Form a local outdoor activity group

3155. Participate in political campaigns

3156. Attend a local budget committee meeting

3157. Form a computer group for local senior citizens

3158. Help coach Little League or other youth sports—even if you don't have a kid playing

3159. Help run the snack bar at the Little League field

3160. Form a tool lending library with neighbors and share ladders, snow blowers, etc.

3161. Start a lunch gathering or a discussion group with co-workers

3162. Offer to rake a neighbor's yard or shovel his/her walk

3163. Start or join a carpool

3164. Employers: give employees time (e.g., 3 days per year) to work on civic projects

3165. Plan a "Walking Tour" of a local historic area

3166. Eat breakfast at a local gathering spot on Saturdays

3167. Have family dinners and read to your children

3168. Run for public office

3169. Host a block party or a holiday open house

3170. Start a fix-it group—friends willing to help each other clean, paint, garden, etc.

3171. Offer to serve on a town committee

3172. Join the volunteer fire department

3173. Go to church or temple or walk outside with your children—talk to them about why it's important

3174. If you grow tomatoes, plant extra for an lonely elder neighbor—better yet, ask him/her to teach you and others how to can the extras

3175. Ask a single diner to share your table for lunch

3176. Stand at a major intersection holding a sign for your favorite candidate

3177. Persuade a local restaurant to have a designated "meet people" table

3178. Host a potluck supper before your Town Meeting

3179. Take dance lessons with a friend

3180. Say "thanks" to public servants—police, firefighters, town clerk, etc.

3181. Fight to keep essential local services in the downtown area–your post office, police station, school, etc.

3182. Join a nonprofit board of directors

3183. Gather a group to clean up a local park or cemetery

3184. When somebody says "government stinks," suggest they help fix it

3185. Turn off the TV and talk with friends or family

3186. Hold a neighborhood barbecue

3187. Bake cookies for new neighbors or work colleagues

3188. Plant tree seedlings along your street with neighbors and rotate care for them

3189. Volunteer at the library

3190. Form or join a bowling team

3191. Return a lost wallet or appointment book

3192. Use public transportation and start talking with those you regularly see

3193. Ask neighbors for help and reciprocate

3194. Go to a local folk or crafts festival

3195. Call an old friend

3196. Sign up for a class and meet your classmates

3197. Accept or extend an invitation

3198. Say hello to strangers

3199. Log off and go to the park

3200. Ask a new person to join a group for a dinner or an evening

3201. Host a pot luck meal or participate in them

3202. Volunteer to drive someone

3203. Say hello when you spot an acquaintance in a store

3204. Host a movie night

3205. Exercise together or take walks with friends or family

3206. Assist with or create your town or neighborhood's newsletter

3207. Collect oral histories from older town residents

3208. Join a book club discussion or get the group to discuss local issues

3209. Volunteer to deliver Meals-on-Wheels in your neighborhood

3210. Start a children's story hour at your local library

3211. Be real. Be humble. Acknowledge others' self-worth

3212. Greet people

3213. Join in to help carry something heavy

3214. Plan a reunion of family, friends, or those with whom you had a special connection

3215. Take in the programs at your local library

3216. Read the local news faithfully

3217. Buy a grill and invite others over for a meal

3218. Fix it even if you didn't break it

3219. Pick it up even if you didn't drop it

3220. Attend a public meeting

3221. Go with friends or colleagues to a ball game (and root, root, root for the home team!)

3222. Help scrape ice off a neighbor's car, put chains on the tires or shovel it out

3223. Hire young people for odd jobs

3224. Start a tradition

3225. Share your snow blower

3226. Help jump-start someone's car

3227. Join a project that includes people from all walks of life

3228. Sit on your stoop

3229. Be nice when you drive

3230. Make gifts of time

3231. Buy a big hot tub

3232. Volunteer at your local neighborhood school

3233. Offer to help out at your local recycling center

3234. Send a "thank you" letter to the Editor about a person or event that helped build community

3235. When inspired, write personal notes to friends and neighbors

3236. Attend gallery openings

3237. Organize a town-wide yard sale

3238. Invite friends or colleagues to help with a home renovation or home building project

3239. Join or start a local mall-walking group and have coffee together afterwards

3240. Build a neighborhood playground

3241. Become a story-reader or baby-rocker at a local child-care center or neighborhood pre-school

3242. Contra dance or two-step

3243. Help kids on your street construct a lemonade stand

3244. Open the door for someone who has his or her hands full

3245. Say hi to those in elevators

3246. Offer to watch your neighbor's home or apartment while they are away

3247. Organize a fitness/health group with your friends or coworkers

3248. Hang out at the town dump and chat with your neighbors as you sort your trash at the Recycling Center

3249. Take pottery classes with your children or parent(s)

3250. See if your neighbor needs anything when you run to the store

3251. Ask to see a friend's family photos

3252. Join groups (e.g. arts, sports, religion) likely to lead to making new friends of different race or ethnicity, different social class or bridging across other dimensions

Working With Four Legs or Wings and a Beak

3253. Spay and neuter your pets

3254. Never buy an animal from a pet shop

3255. Never give an animal as a gift

3256. Never ignore stray animals on the streets. They can become victims of disease, starvation, and abuse

3257. Support your local animal shelter

3258. Adopt your pets from a shelter

3259. If you prefer purebreds, make sure they do not come from a puppy/kitty mill

3260. Report abuse. Call the local humane society if you witness animal cruelty

3261. Keep collars and tags on dogs and cats

3262. Have a secure fence for dogs

3263. Hold a door-to-door campaign to collect unused and used pet items (leashes, food bowls, blankets, canned dog or cat food, etc.) and donate to your local animal shelter

3264. Use natural cleaners. Animals are easily poisoned in the house

3265. Train your dog to be social, in a humane way

3266. Keep your pets in shape—provide exercise opportunities, good nutrition, and play toys

3267. Educate yourself about your pets and meet the needs of the breed

3268. Groom your animals to keep skin healthy

3269. Vaccinate your animals on schedule

3270. Choose food that is right for your pet—less chemicals, better food

3271. Join wildlife protection organizations

3272. Buy cruelty-free consumer products

3273. Call and write companies that currently test products with animals

3274. Do not buy products that contain animal ingredients

3275. Create a wildlife sanctuary in your backyard

3276. Don't feed wildlife

3277. Recycle Christmas trees

3278. Deter ants with spices—ants won't cross cream of tartar, red chili powder, paprika, or dried peppermint

3279. Use bay leaves to keep cockroaches and moths at bay

3280. Use an alternative to mothballs—cedar chips work well

3281. Don't kill spiders—put them outside

3282. Support eco-tourism—watching wildlife is better than hunting them

3283. Teach respect for animals

3284. Support your children's connection to animals

3285. Do not buy imported exotic animals or birds

Simple Ways to Advocate for Animals

3286. Wear "pro-veg" buttons, t-shirts or hats

3287. Take advantage of social-media sites to spread the word

3288. Add an animal-friendly message to your voice mail

3289. Add an animal-friendly message to your email signature

3290. Use charity search engines that donate to animal organizations

3291. Bring a batch of vegan cookies or brownies to work or school

3292. Use animal-friendly user names when posting comments on blogs

3293. Become a vegetarian

3294. Petition your school cafeteria to offer vegetarian and vegan options to the meal plans

3295. Keep a few leaflets with you to pass out

Ways to Help Abandoned Furry Friends

3296. Transport a dog

3297. Donate a dog bed or towels or other bedding items

3298. Donate MONEY

3299. Donate a Kong? A Nylabone? A Hercules?

3300. Donate a crate

3301. Donate an x-pen or baby gates

3302. Donate a leash

3303. Donate a collar

3304. Donate some treats or a bag of food

3305. Donate a halti or promise collar or a gentle leader

3306. Walk a dog

3307. Groom a dog

3308. Donate some grooming supplies (shampoos, combs, brushes, etc.)

3309. Volunteer to help a local shelter identify breeds or help with rescues

3310. Make a few phone calls

3311. Mail out pet adoption applications to people who've requested them

3312. Provide local vet clinics with contact information for educational materials on responsible pet ownership

3313. Drive a dog to and from vet appointments

3314. Donate long distance calling cards

3315. Donate the use of your scanner or digital camera

3316. Attend public education days and try to educate people on responsible pet ownership

3317. Donate a raffle item if your club is holding a fundraiser

3318. Donate flea shampoo and preventatives (Advantage, etc.)

3319. Donate heart worm pills

3320. Donate a canine first-aid kit

3321. Provide a shoulder to cry on when the rescue person is overwhelmed

3322. Pay the boarding fees to board a dog for a week or two

3323. Be a Santi-paws foster parent to give a foster parent a break for a few hours or days

3324. Clip coupons for dog food or treats

3325. Bake some homemade doggie biscuits

3326. Make book purchases through Amazon via a website that contributes commissions earned to a rescue group

3327. Host rescue photos with an information link on your website

3328. Donate time to take good photos of foster dogs for adoption flyers, etc.

3329. Conduct a home visit or accompany a rescue person on the home visit

3330. Go with rescue person to the vet to help if there is more than one dog

3331. Have a yard sale and donate the money to rescue

3332. Be a volunteer to do rescue in your area

3333. Take advantage of a promotion on the web or store offering a free ID tag. Instead of getting it for your own dog, have the tag inscribed with the animal shelter's name and phone number

3334. Talk to all your friends about adopting and fostering rescue dogs

3335. Donate vet services or help by donating a spay or neuter or vaccinations

3336. Interview vets to encourage them to offer discounts to rescues

3337. Write a column for your local newspaper or club newsletter on dogs currently looking for homes or ways to help rescue

3338. Take photos of dogs available for adoption for use by the animal shelter

3339. Maintain websites showing dogs available

3340. Help organize and run fundraising events

3341. Help maintain the paperwork files associated with each dog, or enter the information into a database

3342. Tattoo ID information on a rescued dog

3343. Microchip a rescued dog

3344. Loan your carpet steam-cleaner to someone who has fostered a dog that was sick or marked in the house

3345. Donate a bottle of bleach or other cleaning products

3346. Donate or lend a portable dog run to someone who doesn't have a quarantine area for quarantining a dog that has an unknown vaccination history and has been in a shelter

3347. Drive the foster's children to an activity so the foster can take the dog to obedience class

3348. Use your video camera to film a rescue dog in action

3349. Pay the cost of taking a dog to obedience class

3350. Be the one to take the dog to its obedience class

3351. Go to the foster home once a week with your children and dogs to help socialize the dog

3352. Help the foster clean up the yard (yes, we also have to scoop what those foster dogs poop)

3353. Offer to test the foster dog with cats

3354. Pay for the dog to be groomed or take the dog to a do-it-yourself groomer

3355. Bring the foster dinner so the he or she doesn't have to cook

3356. Pay a house-cleaning service to do the spring cleaning for someone who fosters dogs

3357. Lend your artistic talents to your club's newsletter with fundraising ideas and t-shirt designs

3358. Donate printer paper, envelopes and stamps to your club

3359. Go with a rescue person to the vet if a foster dog needs to be euthanized

3360. Go to local shelters and meet with shelter staff about identifying breeds. Provide photos and information showing the different types and color combinations of each breed

3361. Go to local businesses and solicit donations for a club's fundraising event

3362. Offer to try and help owners be better pet owners by holding a grooming seminar

3363. Help pet owners be better pet owners by being available to answer training questions

3364. Loan a crate if a dog needs to travel by air

3365. Put together an owner's manual for those who adopt rescued dogs of your breed

3366. Provide post-adoption follow up or support

3367. Donate a coupon for a free car wash or gas or inside cleaning of a vehicle

3368. Pay for an ad in your local/metropolitan paper to help place rescue dogs

3369. Volunteer to screen calls for that ad

3370. Get some friends together to build/repair pens for a foster home

3371. Microchip your own pups if you are a breeder, and register the chips so if your dogs ever come into rescue, you can be contacted to take responsibility for your pup

3372. Donate a small percentage of the sale of each pup to rescue if you are a breeder

3373. Buy two of those really neat dog-items you "have to have" and donate one to Rescue

3374. Make financial arrangements in your will to cover the cost of caring for your dogs after you are gone—so Rescue won't have to

3375. Make a bequest in your will to your local or national Rescue

3376. Donate your professional services as an accountant or lawyer

3377. Donate other services if you run your own business

3378. Donate the use of a vehicle if you own a car dealership

3379. Loan your cell phone (and cover costs for any calls) to someone driving a rescued dog

3380. Donate your *used* dog dryer when you get a new one

3381. Let rescue know when you'll be flying and that you'd be willing to be a rescued dog's escort

3382. Donate a doggy seatbelt

3383. Donate a grid for a van or other vehicle

3384. Organize a rescued dog picnic or other event to reunite the rescued dogs that have been placed

3385. Donate other types of doggy toys that might be safe for rescued dogs

3386. Donate a roll-a-treat or Buster cube

3387. Donate clickers or a training video

3388. Donate materials for a quarantine area at a foster's home

3389. Donate sheets of linoleum or other flooring material to put under crates to protect the foster's floor

3390. Donate an engraving tool to make ID tags for each of the rescued dogs

3391. Remember that rescuing a dog involves the effort and time of many people. Make yourself available on an emergency basis to do whatever is needed

3392. Create an adopt-a-pet website with pictures of available animals

3393. Do something not listed above to help rescue

A Better You

3394. Hold a baby. It makes everything right with the world

3395. Pray—God really listens

3396. Sing—what better way to praise God?

3397. Attend services at a church other than your own

3398. Climb a tree

3399. Stargaze from a roof

3400. Mentally pick a number. Physically smile at that many people today (whether you know them or not!)

3401. Go bike riding with your kids

3402. Take some time to discover and develop your favorite personal talent or gift. Then, create a fundraiser for charity that somehow uses that talent or gift

3403. Participate at meetings

3404. Wake up early to watch the sunrise

3405. Take a spontaneous road trip

3406. Sing in the shower

3407. Realize that sometimes good enough is good enough

3408. Get into a mud fight

3409. Be what you pretend to be

3410. Organize a drive-in movie event

3411. Whenever possible, spend time with people who are better than you are

3412. Travel as a missionary/ social justice worker

3413. Stand up for a just cause with your actions

3414. Tithe to your church

3415. Subscribe to the *Liguorian* magazine

3416. Take a nature hike

3417. Be someone else's super-model

3418. Visit a cemetery

3419. For today, live in the present

3420. Give up your power

3421. Run toward your fears

3422. Send someone an unexpected complimentary text message

3423. Give a busy mom a "mom's day out" by watching her children for free

3424. Run an errand for someone who is busy

3425. Knowledge, creativity, and positive attitude are contagious; get infected.

3426. Infect others with your positive attitude.

3427. Drive carpool for someone when it is not your turn

3428. Learn how to say "love" in 5 languages

3429. Learn how to say "peace" in 5 languages

3430. Rescue a stray pet

3431. Spend time with someone who does not look like you. Learn from them

3432. Eat only a bowl of rice a day for a week to remember those who do that for most of their lives

3433. Go immediately to be with someone who just found out a special friend or family member died

3434. Work one full day remembering and praying for those who toil harder and earn less. Give this day's earnings to someone who has less than you

3435. Anonymously give cash to someone in need

3436. Listen genuinely and intently to someone who normally annoys you

3437. Visit an ocean and beach to observe God's wondrous expanse

3438. Don't just create to-do lists, create to-un-do lists

3439. Donate airline frequent flyer miles to someone who needs to fly to receive medical treatment

3440. Create and recite a personal mantra

3441. Count your blessings

3442. Do something positive for someone you know

3443. Do something positive for a complete stranger

3444. Do something positive for yourself

3445. Change one behavior to better yourself

3446. Forgive another for a wrong done to you

3447. Forgive yourself for something

3448. Do something that you have been putting off doing

3449. Finish a project that you just can't get finished

3450. Think 3 optimistic thoughts today

3451. Before putting your feet on the floor and getting out of bed in the morning, thank God for your life and the gift of this day

3452. Live the entire day as if your glass is half full

3453. Use God's works to uplift someone

3454. Plant a vegetable garden

3455. Plant flowers in the spring

3456. Sleep outside under the stars

3457. Visit a mosque

3458. Visit a synagogue

3459. Commit to memory a new prayer

3460. Commit to memory a favorite poem

3461. Read a book on world religions

3462. Attend church regularly

3463. Attend an outdoor mass

3464. Write and say a peace prayer

3465. Build a grotto

3466. Doodle

3467. Sing in your church choir

3468. Sing in your church if you're not in the choir

3469. Attend a posadas service

3470. Attend a seder meal

3471. Learn something about the history of your house of worship

3472. Learn something about church history

3473. Join a Corpus Christi procession

3474. Say grace before and after meals

3475. Place a statue of Mary or Saint Francis in your yard

3476. Go on retreat

3477. Go on a silent retreat

3478. Practice silence for a whole day

3479. Attend a mission trip

3480. Erect a peace pole

3481. Communicate without words

3482. Obtain a spiritual director

3483. Keep a Journal

3484. Spend an entire month without a car

3485. Read and read some more

3486. Write a spiritual poem

3487. Clean out your clothes closet and donate anything you haven't worn in the last 12 months to charity

3488. Tell your parents "thank you." If your parents are deceased, write a thank you letter to them in memory of them

3489. Learn the words and sing the song "Kumbaya My Lord"

3490. Ride a horse on a beach

3491. Attend a musical concert

3492. Indulge in your favor fantasy

3493. Try Karaoke

3494. Spend time at an ashram

3495. Visit a Marian shrine

3496. Try new foods.

3497. Study a foreign language

3498. Spend a day pretending you don't speak English

3499. Enjoy the scenery from the top of the house

3500. Walk El Camino del Santiago

3501. Attend an ecumenical prayer service

3502. Indulge in a full-body massage

3503. Have your house blessed

3504. Spoil your kids every once in a while

3505. Clip coupons

3506. Exchange places with your spouse for a day

3507. Write a life plan

3508. Train for a marathon and then run it

3509. Learn to sew

3510. Have your pet blessed

3511. Invite your friends over for a slumber party

3512. Make your own bread

3513. Find and develop your own hidden talents

3514. Trust yourself

3515. Attend service at a church in a foreign country

3516. Just breathe

3517. Visit the Shrine of Our Lady of Lourdes in France

3518. Walk the Stations of the Cross at the Shrine of Our Lady of Lourdes

3519. Visit Vatican City

3520. Start a conversation with a complete stranger

3521. Barter your skills

3522. Stop making New Year's resolutions unless you know you can keep them

3523. Vote, every time

3524. Test drive new cars

3525. Recycle

3526. Donate prayer books and Bibles to inmates in a prison

3527. Pump iron

3528. Drive around and view Christmas lights and decorations on homes

3529. Clean up someone else's mess

3530. Recognize your own addictions

3531. Create new family legends

3532. Laugh out loud, every day

3533. Sponsor a child in a charity fundraiser such as the MDA's jump-a-thon

3534. Coordinate a "walkathon" team for a needy cause

3535. Buy a box of girl scout cookies

3536. Spend a month without television

3537. Be present for a birth

3538. Be present for a death

3539. Meet your spouse at a hotel

3540. Buy a gift subscription to the *Liguorian* magazine for a friend or relative

3541. Stop and buy a glass of lemonade at a child's corner lemonade stand

3542. Spend Thanksgiving Day preparing and serving food at a food pantry

3543. Meditate for 30 minutes each day for one week

3544. Be part of the crowd

3545. Stay an extra day on vacation or with family

3546. Lose a game to your spouse and children

3547. Leave the bed unmade and dishes in the sink

3548. Lobby for legislation on something you believe in

3549. Get a professional makeover

3550. Be childlike, but not childish

3551. Learn the Heimlich maneuver

3552. Knit a sweater

3553. Write a letter to your congressional representative supporting a social justice issue or moral cause

3554. View a sunrise on the coast of the Atlantic Ocean

3555. View a sunset on the coast of the Pacific Ocean

3556. Visit a famous church or temple

3557. Build and hang a bird house

3558. Attend a bat/bar mitzvah or a quinceañeras

3559. Attend a wedding performed in a different faith

3560. Climb and play in a tree house

3561. Sleep in a tree house

3562. Climb a mountain

3563. Drive down Route 66

3564. Ride a cable car in San Francisco

3565. Go lobster fishing in Maine

3566. Go fly fishing

3567. Make homemade ice cream

3568. Go to Mardi Gras

3569. Visit a veterans memorial cemetery

3570. Visit Washington, DC

3571. Go to an opera

3572. See the Grand Canyon

3573. View Old Faithful in Yellowstone National Park

3574. Go white-water rafting

3575. Watch an eclipse

3576. Write a haiku poem

3577. Play cards with an elderly person

3578. Plan a scavenger hunt for kids

3579. Participate in a scavenger hunt

3580. Sell something on eBay

3581. Work for a political campaign

3582. Wear a blindfold for 24 hours

3583. Go ice skating in Rockefeller Center

3584. Swim in the ocean

3585. Float in the Great Salt Lake

3586. Go deep see fishing

3587. Milk a cow

3588. Develop and stick to a 30-day exercise plan

3589. Ask a friend to walk with you regularly

3590. Pull a tooth

3591. Be a secret angel

3592. Be the tooth fairy

3593. Volunteer at an animal shelter

3594. Paint a picture

3595. Put a 1000-piece puzzle together with a friend or relative

3596. Swim with dolphins

3597. Donate books to a library

3598. Establish a scholarship fund

3599. Help pay the private-school tuition for someone who needs help

3600. Ride a two-seater bike

3601. Walk in a parade

3602. Visit a botanical garden

3603. Make a snow angel

3604. Throw a surprise party for someone

3605. Observe a full moon

3606. Go snorkeling

3607. Shovel snow off your neighbor's driveway

3608. Play hopscotch with kids

3609. Help teach Sunday School class for kids

3610. Play jump rope with kids

3611. Help at summer camp

3612. Go apple picking

3613. Make applesauce and share it with your neighbors

3614. Teach a child to tie their shoe

3615. Play sidewalk chalk with kids

3616. Walk a dog

3617. Be a secret Santa

3618. Pay someone's past due utility bill

3619. Create a "101 goals in 1000 Days" List

3620. Buy a house

3621. Contact an old friend

3622. Run for school board

3623. Attend 10 toastmaster meetings

3624. Begin a blog

3625. Can at least 20 jars of salsa or tomato sauce for winter

3626. Drink only water as a beverage for a year

3627. Complete a book proposal

3628. Learn another language

Work on Quality & Quantity of Life

3629. Eat small meals

3630. Serve breakfast to your family

3631. Cut calories

3632. Increase proteins

3633. Don't overeat

3634. Avoid fad diets

3635. Go natural—eat organic, use natural products

3636. Eat balanced meals

3637. Avoid fast foods

3638. Drink plenty of water

3639. Limit artificial additives

3640. Reduce the number of sodas your children drink

3641. Eat garlic

3642. Eliminate white sugar

3643. Drink green tea

3644. Add "superfoods" to your diet—broccoli, spinach, tomatoes, mushrooms, etc.,

3645. Take the stairs, and teach your kids to do the same

3646. Take a walk every day

3647. Ride a bike, and encourage your kids to do the same

3648. Make yard work a family affair

3649. Lean Tai Chi

3650. Swim and teach your kids to swim

3651. Learn to breathe

3652. Get regular medical check-ups

3653. Get regular dental check-ups

3654. See your eye doctor

3655. Protect your skin and that of your children with sunscreen and moisturizer

3656. Drink alcohol in moderation

3657. Drink red wine

3658. Stop smoking and teach your children not to smoke

3659. Laugh—a lot

3660. Practice meditation and prayer daily

3661. Be grateful

3662. Remain flexible

3663. Be adventurous

3664. Always keep learning

3665. Overcome bad moods

3666. Think positively

3667. Treat disease, including depression

3668. Wear seat belts

3669. Use sports helmets

3670. No drinking (or doing drugs) and driving

3671. Don't do illegal drugs—period

3672. Install smoke detectors

3673. Lock up your house

3674. Install safety alarms

3675. Install handrails

3676. Install safety gates for kids

3677. Practice smart home safety

3678. Teach everyone how to get out of the house in an emergency

3679. Manage stress

3680. Travel and see the world

3681. Sleep regularly—and remember, kids need even more sleep than you do

3682. Have friends and include children in that circle of friends

3683. Adopt a pet

3684. Have alone time

3685. Balance your work and family

3686. Teach your family to eat slowly and enjoy the meal

3687. Take up an art—paint, write, dance, sculpt

3688. Try new foods and introduce your children to new cuisine

3689. Take up a hobby

3690. Attend art events—go to a concert, a play, a museum

3691. Never give yourself an "out" of I'm too old

Build Community in Less Than 30 Minutes

3692. Take a garbage bag with you while taking a walk in the park

3693. Shop with locally owned businesses

3694. Attend a local festival or other events

3695. Write a letter to local elected officials encouraging them for making good decisions for the community

3696. Put a potted plant on your front porch

3697. Run for office

3698. Look for opportunities to contribute your work skills to community service

3699. Become a volunteer firefighter

3700. Become a volunteer crossing guard at school

3701. Vote

3702. Vote for the person, not the party

3703. Encourage your employer to support local events

3704. Join and support civic organizations

3705. Attend city council meetings

3706. Attend county board meetings

3707. Keep your yard clean

3708. Volunteer for a health fair

Celebrate Multiculturalism

3709. Recognize, understand and appreciate ways in which your own racial, cultural, ethnic background has contributed to your character and personality

3710. Be careful about the "messages" you send

3711. Practice "trying on" different ideas

3712. Research materials that offer insights into another culture

3713. Go to a movie created by someone of a different culture

3714. Help a girl or woman in your life do something they thought impossible

3715. Smile and say hello first—even if you're pretty sure the other person won't respond

3716. Talk to others about current events

3717. Participate in interfaith religious services

3718. Participate in intergenerational activities

3719. Get acquainted with someone from a different country

3720. Get a pen pal that lives a world away

3721. Learn about your own family history

3722. Volunteer to do something that puts you in contact with people who are different from you

3723. Speak up when you see someone being treated unfairly

3724. Be aware of how language and terms describe people of different races, religions, etc.

3725. Don't make assumptions about people based on their race or religion

3726. Decorate your home that reflects your heritage and invite others to learn about it

3727. Lobby public offices to develop strong and clear human rights policies

3728. Attend a rally to support peace, equality and fairness

3729. Travel the Black Heritage Trail

3730. Visit the Museum of Afro-American History

3731. Learn your country's history

3732. Visit the American Indian Museum

3733. Learn another language

3734. Celebrate holidays that are not part of your own heritage—follow the traditions of that holiday

3735. Attend an art exhibit or music program featuring art from another country

3736. Learn about support organizations supporting peace and human rights

3737. Encourage children to be activists for social justice

3738. Be willing to tolerate discomfort while confronting your own stereotypes

3739. Ask candidates about their stance concerning human rights and multicultural issues

3740. Don't join clubs and organizations that discriminate

3741. When planning civic events, make sure people of all races, ethnicities, abilities and class are welcome and able to participate

3742. Challenge "macho" stereotypes

3743. Make an effort to pronounce names correctly

3744. Learn local customs of places you visit

3745. Volunteer to give a classroom program on your cultural background

3746. Share stories of your family and heritage

3747. Think about all the factors that affect the way you think about the world

3748. Ask your children to describe themselves

3749. Teach your children personal pride

3750. Know you can make a difference

3751. Do not tolerate age discrimination

3752. Be conscious of the ways you treat boys and girls differently

3753. Advocate multicultural education

3754. Thank a teacher for his/her work at teaching tolerance

3755. Think about differences that are invisible, such as learning styles

3756. Express ideas, not truths

3757. Help someone from another country feel welcome in yours

3758. Be aware of the messages media sends in regards to race, religion, culture, etc.

3759. Encourage young people who are trying to make a difference

3760. Volunteer and service on committees working at hiring a diverse staff

3761. Acknowledge racism exists

3762. Notice how female, elderly, and overweight people are portrayed in movies, cartoons, television, and in general conversations

3763. Challenge your assumptions about people in wheelchairs

3764. Point out prejudice when it happens

3765. Learn about and support school policies that condemn bullying and harassment of all kinds

3766. Take note of our own actions

Helping Your Parents/Grandparents

3767. Check on their nutrition

3768. Locate a geriatric-care manager

3769. Alter the house to fit their needs

3770. Encourage them to keep friendships

3771. Sign up for door-to-door shuttle service

3772. Have meals delivered, if necessary

3773. Provide transportation for friends to visit them in their home

3774. Order a 24/7 medical alert system

3775. Shop for products that will make daily life easier

3776. Visit and call often

3777. Always include them in family festivities

3778. Ask if they want to accompany you while you run your errands just to get out of the house

3779. If a friend of theirs dies, offer to go to the wake or funeral with them

3780. Set up a regular lunch or dinner—every Tuesday, the third Sunday of every month—otherwise, you'll suddenly realize it's been six months since you've see them

3781. Buy her an ebook reader

3782. Help with estate planning

3783. Talk frankly about eldercare

3784. Organize a grandparent/grandchild retreat

3785. Help with taxes

3786. Listen to their stories, even if you have heard them a hundred times

3787. Give experiences, not sweaters

3788. Sign them up for a health club membership

3789. Give them a Netflix subscription

3790. Maintain a safe living environment for them

3791. Help them with living wills

3792. Accompany them to appointments

3793. Teach them online skills—email, research, blogs, etc.

3794. Keep them involved in activities that are important to them

Be Life's Best Customer Service Representative

3795. Don't let anyone enter your life without a warm greeting

3796. Make everyone feel welcome

3797. Don't single people out because they are alone

3798. Start the conversations

3799. Remain neutral—don't lead the witness

3800. Always present a willingness to help

3801. Offer personal suggestions and favors only when asked

3802. Acquaint yourself with the customs of others

3803. Don't interrupt conversations

3804. When you ask, "How's everything?" listen to the answer and fix what you can

3805. Never say "I don't know" say "I'll find out"

3806. Separate the person from the problem

3807. Never touch without permission

3808. Never mention what your favorite dessert is

3809. Never acknowledge one person over another

3810. Turning on the charm at tip time is a no-no

3811. Address everyone as you would wish to be addressed

3812. Respect privacy

3813. Distinguish between means (method) and ends (result)

3814. Develop self-sufficiency

3815. Know procedures

3816. Use common courtesy

3817. If there is a service charge, alert others

3818. Don't double-order

3819. Don't bring judgment with the ketchup

3820. Make sure there is room at the table for everyone

3821. Don't leave the glass empty

3822. It's all about the appetizers

3823. Don't ignore one guest in favor of another

3824. Don't blame the chef because the order is wrong

3825. Rushing life's customers is just rude

3826. Understand that everyone has trouble making decisions now and then

3827. Specials of the day, whether written or spoken, should have prices clearly displayed

3828. Remember that no one is finished until they are finished

3829. Do not disappear

3830. Never ask for payment until payment is due

3831. Never make people wait for the check

3832. Be a guest at your own table

3833. Ask about allergies

3834. Open the door to life, and hold the door for others

3835. Answer requests with a smile

3836. If someone complains about the music, be willing to play another song

3837. Never hover long enough to make people feel they are being watched

3838. Understand personal space

3839. Don't show frustration

3840. Guests, like servers, come in all packages

3841. If someone goes ga-ga over something you made— give them the recipe or pattern, etc.

3842. Be willing to dance with a wallflower

3843. Be willing to dance alone

3844. Don't take the plate away while someone is still eating

3845. Everyone is entitled to a clean glass of water

3846. Offer your guests bread and wine

3847. Never assume people want what you are offering

3848. Never forget that the most unhappy customers is your greatest source of learning

Improve Community Health Care

3849. Work to enforce accountability among medical staff

3850. Monitor the goals of community health care

3851. Organize a group to gather information on services provided

3852. Report your findings to officials

3853. Volunteer for an oversight board

3854. Contribute time and money where needed

3855. Work with community leaders to develop benchmarks

3856. Petition for budget consideration at the local level

3857. Provide basic services such as clerical skills to the office and to clients

3858. Support new procedures

3859. Help with grant writing

3860. Donate a building

3861. Provide transportation to those in need

3862. Sponsor health fairs

3863. Campaign for candidates with a health care agenda that matches yours

3864. Volunteer for flu shot clinics

3865. Advocate for the sick in the community

3866. Get paramedic training

3867. Don't abuse health care systems

3868. Promote health issues

Educating Students of Tomorrow

3869. Remember "one size does not fit all"

3870. Live by our beliefs

3871. Remember that content is concepts, principles and skills that are conveyed to students

3872. Processes help students make sense of the content

3873. Make things crystal clear

3874. Be as flexible as possible in a whole class situation

3875. Motivate students to learn

3876. Involve students of all levels in the process

3877. Create incentives to learn

3878. Help train teachers

3879. Build behavior skills

3880. Work on social behavior problems early

3881. Reduce social barriers

3882. Recognize students as stakeholders in the process

3883. Provide kids with simple learning opportunities

3884. Volunteer tutoring skills

3885. Provide financial incentives for educators

3886. Provide financial incentives for students

3887. Offer second chances

3888. Reach out to dropouts

3889. Start an English As a Second Language class at church

3890. Start literacy programs

3891. Teach job-searching skills

3892. Start a job-training program

3893. Provide vocational school opportunities

3894. Start a scholarship

3895. Volunteer for Teach for America (www.teachforamerica. org)

3896. Promote community partnerships

3897. Get parents involved

3898. Provide adult education

3899. Use online resources

3900. Teach online skills to students

3901. Encourage online classwork

Support Your School

3902. Tell stories to children

3903. Listen to children read

3904. Conduct flash card drills

3905. Provide individual help

3906. Assist in learning centers

3907. Help contact parents

3908. Work in a clinic

3909. Work in the library

3910. Check out audiovisual equipment

3911. Run copy machine for school office and teachers

3912. Practice vocabulary with non-English–speaking students

3913. Make instructional games

3914. Play instructional games

3915. Play games at recess

3916. Prepare visual materials for teachers

3917. Assist with visual tests

3918. Make bulletin boards

3919. Help with book fairs

3920. Reinforce Dolch words (www.dolchsightwords.org)

3921. Supervise at listening stations

3922. Make props for plays

3923. Make costumes

3924. Set up and run an in-school bookstore

3925. Gather resource materials

3926. Escort children to bathrooms

3927. Work on perceptual activities

3928. Prepare teaching materials

3929. Discuss careers and hobbies

3930. Reinforce the alphabet

3931. Reinforce numeral recognition

3932. Drill recognition of color words

3933. Help children with motor skill problems

3934. Assist in building social skills

3935. Make puppets

3936. Dramatize a story

3937. Play and teach a musical instrument

3938. Help with handwriting practices

3939. Drill spelling words

3940. Help with hearing and vision screenings

3941. Make reading carrels from cardboard boxes

3942. Compile a guide to community resources

3943. Help with classroom parties

3944. Check out and return equipment borrowed from other facilities

3945. Organize and maintain a classroom library

3946. Make or mend books, posters, workbooks, learning games or toys used by students

3947. Make graphs and charts for students

3948. Make flashcards

3949. Make picture-word cards

3950. Translate plays and other materials for bilingual instruction projects

3951. Distribute books

3952. Distribute school notices

3953. Set up materials for teacher presentations

3954. Assist during school registration

3955. Alphabetize materials for various school files

3956. Help small children with coats

3957. Take new students on building tour

3958. Record or write down the stories children tell

3959. Assist with creative writing projects

3960. Assist in using educational toys and games

3961. Aid students with science experiments

3962. Aid students with art projects

3963. Aid students with any special activities

3964. Assist individuals and groups with enrichment instructional projects

3965. Assist individual students with independent study or follow-up work

3966. Work in the teacher workroom

3967. Work at the school's sign-up desk

3968. Recruit additional volunteers

3969. Go on field trips with classes

3970. Sell school supplies

3971. Serve on the PTA board

3972. Join PTO

3973. Pass along information on workshops

3974. Volunteer in the cafeteria

3975. Support fundraising efforts

3976. Be a teacher's aid

3977. Be a substitute teacher

3978. Help physical-education teachers on field days

3979. Organize a school family picnic

3980. Help in school office

3981. Help in computer lab

3982. Serve at teacher luncheons

3983. Be a playground monitor

Show Kids You Care

3984. Notice them

3985. Smile a lot

3986. Acknowledge them

3987. Learn their names

3988. Seek them out

3989. Remember their birthday

3990. Ask them about themselves

3991. Look in their eyes when you talk to them

3992. Listen to them

3993. Play with them

3994. Read aloud together

3995. Giggle together

3996. Be nice

3997. Say yes a lot

3998. Tell them their feelings are OK

3999. Set boundaries that keep them safe

4000. Be honest

4001. Be yourself

4002. Listen to their stories

4003. Hug them

4004. Forget your worries sometimes and concentrate only on them

4005. Notice when they're acting differently

4006. Present options when they seek your counsel

4007. Play outside together

4008. Surprise them

4009. Stay with them when they're afraid

4010. Invite them over for juice

4011. Suggest better behaviors when they act out

4012. Feed them when they're hungry

4013. Delight in their discoveries

4014. Share their excitement

4015. Send them a letter or postcard

4016. Follow them when they lead

4017. Notice when they're absent

4018. Call them to say hello

4019. Hide surprises for them to find

4020. Give them space when they need it

4021. Contribute to their collections

4022. Discuss their dreams and nightmares

4023. Laugh at their jokes

4024. Be relaxed

4025. Kneel, squat, or sit so you're at their eye level

4026. Answer their questions

4027. Tell them how terrific they are

4028. Create a tradition with them and keep it

4029. Learn what they have to teach

4030. Use your ears more than your mouth

4031. Make yourself available

4032. Show up at their concerts, games, and events

4033. Find a common interest

4034. Hold hands during a walk

4035. Apologize when you've done something wrong

4036. Listen to their favorite music with them

4037. Keep the promises you make

4038. Wave and smile when you part

4039. Display their artwork in your home

4040. Thank them

4041. Point out what you like about them

4042. Clip magazine pictures or articles that interest them

4043. Give them lots of compliments

4044. Catch them doing something right

4045. Encourage win-win solutions

4046. Give them your undivided attention

4047. Ask for their opinion

4048. Have fun together

4049. Be curious with them

4050. Introduce them to your friends and family

4051. Tell them how much you like being with them

4052. Let them solve most of their own problems

4053. Meet their friends

4054. Meet their parents

4055. Let them tell you how they feel

4056. Help them become an expert at something

4057. Be excited when you see them

4058. Tell them about yourself

4059. Let them act their age

4060. Praise more; criticize less

4061. Be consistent

4062. Admit when you make a mistake

4063. Give them a special nickname

4064. Marvel at what they can do

4065. Tell them how proud you are of them

4066. Pamper them

4067. Unwind together

4068. Be happy

4069. Ask them to help you

4070. Support them

4071. Applaud their successes

4072. Deal with problems and conflicts while they're still small

4073. Chaperon a dance

4074. Tell them stories in which they are the hero

4075. Believe in them

4076. Nurture them with good food

4077. Be flexible

4078. Delight in their uniqueness

4079. Let them make mistakes

4080. Notice when they grow

4081. Wave and honk when you drive by them

4082. Give them immediate feedback

4083. Include them in conversations

4084. Respect them

4085. Join in their adventures

4086. Visit their schools

4087. Help them learn something new

4088. Be understanding when they have a difficult day

4089. Give them good choices

4090. Respect the choices they make

4091. Be silly together

4092. Hang out together

4093. Make time

4094. Inspire their creativity

4095. Accept them as they are

4096. Become their advocate

4097. Appreciate their personality

4098. Talk openly with them

4099. Tolerate their interruptions

4100. Trust them

4101. Share a secret

4102. Write a chalk message on their sidewalk

4103. Create a safe, open environment

4104. Be available

4105. Cheer their accomplishments

4106. Encourage them to help others

4107. Tackle new tasks together

4108. Believe what they say

4109. Help them take a stand and stand with them

4110. Daydream with them

4111. Do what they like to do

4112. Make decisions together

4113. Magnify their magnificence

4114. Build something together

4115. Encourage them to think big

4116. Celebrate their firsts and lasts, such as the first day of school

4117. Go places together

4118. Welcome their suggestions

4119. Visit them when they're sick

4120. Tape record a message for them

4121. Help them learn from mistakes

4122. Be sincere

4123. Introduce them to people of excellence

4124. Tell them what you expect of them

4125. Give them your phone number

4126. Introduce them to new experiences

4127. Share a meal together

4128. Talk directly together

4129. Be spontaneous

4130. Expect their best; don't expect perfection

4131. Empower them to help and be themselves

4132. Love them, no matter what

Time in a Bottle

4133. Put your goals in writing

4134. Focus on the objectives, not on activities

4135. Try to achieve one important objective daily

4136. Question all your activities

4137. Get rid of at least one time waster in your life each month

4138. Make a daily to-do list

4139. Accomplish important things first

4140. Set time limits on tasks

4141. Make sure the first hour of your day is productive

4142. Do things right the first time

4143. Block out an hour a day of uninterrupted time

Finding Your Own Passion

4144. Explore what you are good at

4145. Ask yourself what really excites you

4146. Look at your reading habits for hidden interests

4147. Analyze your dreams

4148. Ask yourself what you secretly dream of

4149. Learn, ask, take notes

4150. Experiment

4151. Narrow things down to three to five things on your list that truly mean something to you

4152. Banish fear

4153. Make the time to pursue your passion

4154. Explore ways to make a living from that passion

4155. If you could focus on only one thing for the rest of your life, what would it be

Zen Habits

4156. Pray and Meditate daily

4157. Stop addictive behaviors

4158. Take on responsibility

4159. Talk about what is bothering you

4160. Tune into your body

4161. Tune into your mind

4162. Pace yourself

4163. Understand that life is not a bowl of cherries

4164. Break down the questions of what truly matters

4165. Imagine what your life will look like in ten years

4166. Practice self improvement daily

4167. Practice self-help daily

4168. Find out what really matters to you

4169. Drop unnecessary activity

4170. Protect your private time

4171. Accept help

4172. Don't over plan

4173. Nuke laziness

4174. Don't be married to your job

4175. Create realistic expectations

4176. Join a spiritual community

4177. Create opportunities to communicate

4178. Communicate without talking

4179. Use technology to your advantage

4180. Create personal traditions

4181. Control your thoughts

4182. Control your actions

4183. Practice complete openness

4184. Seek to understand every being

4185. Tread lightly

Find Your Hero Within

4186. Take a deep breath and ask yourself what is the right thing to do

4187. Anchor yourself in your own values

4188. Turn fear and anxiety into action

4189. Affirm your humanity in the face of inhumanity

4190. Drop your ego and look a the situation clearly

4191. Arm yourself with knowledge, no conjecture

4192. Counter negativity

4193. Take strength knowing that no matter the resolution, you did the best you could

4194. Remember good things come out of bad situations

4195. Laugh out loud and invite others to laugh with you

4196. Remember anyone can be a hero

4197. Find the "hero" in others

4198. Simplify

4199. Find heroes to emulate

4200. Be honest with yourself and others

4201. Heroes come in all shapes, sizes and ages

Recipe for Creativity

4202. Take a warm bath

4203. Go for a drive with the windows open

4204. Order Chinese food and eat it with chopsticks

4205. Ask a child

4206. Create an idea that would get you fired

4207. Paint your bedroom

4208. Consult tarot cards

4209. Gargle

4210. Play football

4211. Sing a show tune on a crowded elevator

4212. How would your favorite uncle solve the problem?

4213. Doodle

4214. Do a crossword puzzle

4215. Pray for a little help

4216. Ask the most creative person you know

4217. Ask the least creative person you know

4218. Go for a Run

4219. Ask your local postal worker

4220. Ice skate

4221. Take a shower with your clothes on

4222. Ask yourself, "What rhymes with orange?"

4223. Talk to your favorite cheerleader about the idea

4224. Breathe slowly

4225. Flip a coin

4226. Mow the lawn

4227. What is the simplest solution?

4228. Do 20 quick push-ups

4229. Go shopping!

4230. Write the alphabet backwards

4231. Build a fort in your office

4232. How would an ant solve the problem

4233. Create a silly solution that rhymes

4234. Make paper airplanes

4235. Use three wishes to solve your challenge

4236. Browse through a bookstore

4237. Take a survey

4238. Go fishing

4239. Go to Vegas, play a lot of craps

4240. Daydream

4241. How would you solve it with an infinite budget?

4242. Write out the problem with your opposite hand

4243. Sing the National Anthem with a cockney accent

4244. Eat dinner

4245. Change your brand of coffee

4246. Wash dishes

4247. Find the solution in the clouds

4248. Swing

4249. Take a nap at your desk

4250. Go bowling

4251. Spin in your chair shouting: "WHOOPEE!"

4252. Eat a snow cone

4253. Contort your face in a strange and unusual ways

4254. High-five yourself

4255. Go camping

4256. Take Spot for a walk

4257. Massage your scalp for 10 minutes

4258. Play musical chairs

4259. Go for a walk in the rain

4260. Pick up something with your toes

4261. Communicate through every means possible

4262. Stand on your head

4263. Stand on someone else's head

4264. Call a psychic hotline, laugh at their predictions

4265. Consume massive amounts of caffeine

4266. More caffeine

4267. Imagine explaining the idea at an awards banquet

4268. Call a friend and speak with an accent

4269. Think about it before you go to sleep

4270. Call mom, she can fix anything

4271. When in doubt, resort to duct tape

4272. Watch slasher movies to boost your creative confidence

4273. Fly a kite

4274. Shake up a can of pop and open it

4275. Go for a walk

4276. Draw a picture of it

4277. Pretend to snorkel

4278. Think like a child

4279. Walk outside and wave to a stranger

4280. Look at the person's paper next to you

4281. Climb a tree

4282. Find a new word in the dictionary

4283. Take an ice cream break

4284. Make a daisy chain

4285. Dance a polka

4286. Play in a toy store

4287. Just don't think about it

4288. Jump on a treadmill

4289. Put your refrigerator contents in alphabetical order

4290. Put your pantry contents in alphabetical order

4291. Pretend like it doesn't matter

4292. Paint with your fingers

4293. Clean your toilet

4294. Lose yourself in your favorite music

4295. Watch old black & white reruns

4296. Listen to bees

4297. Walk in a grocery store—notice clever solutions

4298. Rake the leaves in your yard

4299. Sit outside and count the stars

4300. Ask a think tank

Fashion Forward

4301. Don't be a slave to fashion

4302. Create your own style

4303. Help a friend understand what looks best on her

4304. Hold a Swap-a-Rama to trade outfits with your friends

4305. Paint your shoes

4306. Experiment with colors

4307. Be your own best friend

Things to Do Before You Die

4308. Attend at least one major sporting event: the Super Bowl, the Olympics, the US Open

4309. Throw a huge party and invite every one of your friends

4310. Swim with a dolphin

4311. Skydive

4312. Have your portrait painted

4313. Learn to speak a foreign language and make sure you use it

4314. Go skinny-dipping at midnight in the South of France

4315. Watch the launch of a Space mission

4316. Spend a whole day eating junk food without feeling guilty

4317. Be an extra in a film

4318. Tell someone the story of your life, sparing no details

4319. Make love on a forest floor (but first check for poison oak)

4320. Learn belly dancing

4321. Learn to rollerblade

4322. Own a room with a view

4323. Brew your own beer

4324. Learn how to take a compliment

4325. Buy a round-the-world air ticket and a rucksack, and run away

4326. Grow a beard and leave it for at least a month

4327. Give our mother and her sisters a nature cruise to watch whales

4328. Be a member of the audience in a TV show

4329. Put your name down to be a passenger on the first tourist shuttle to the moon

4330. Send a message in a bottle

4331. Ride a camel into the Australian outback

4332. Dance naked on the solstice

4333. Plant a tree

4334. Learn not to say yes when you really mean no

4335. Write a fan letter to your all-time favorite hero or heroine

4336. Visit the Senate and the House of Representatives to see how Congress really works

4337. Learn to ballroom dance *properly*

4338. Eat jellied eels from a stall in London

4339. Be the boss

4340. Fall deeply in love

4341. Ride the Trans-Siberian Express across Asia

4342. Eat Yak in Mongolia

4343. Write the novel you know you have inside you

4344. Go to Walden Pond and read Thoreau while drifting in a canoe

4345. Stay out all night dancing and go to work the next day without having gone home (just once)

4346. Drink beer at Oktoberfest in Munich

4347. Be someone's mentor

4348. Shower in a waterfall

4349. Ask for a raise

4350. Learn to play a musical instrument with some degree of skill

4351. Be one of the first to take a flight on the new Airbus A380

4352. Spend a night in a haunted house—by yourself

4353. Spend a night in a Pyramid—by yourself

4354. Write down your personal mission statement, follow it, and revise it from time to time

4355. See a lunar eclipse

4356. Spend New Year's on the International Date Line

4357. Get passionate about a cause and spend time helping it, instead of just thinking about it

4358. Experience weightlessness

4359. Sing a great song in front of an audience

4360. Ask someone you've only just met to go on a date

4361. Drive across America from coast to coast

4362. Make a complete and utter fool of yourself

4363. Own one very expensive but absolutely wonderful business suit

4364. Go on a cattle drive

4365. Sleep under the stars

4366. Take a ride on the ten highest roller coasters

4367. Learn how to complain effectively—and do it!

4368. Go wild in Rio during Carnival

4369. Spend a whole day reading a great novel

4370. Forgive your parents

4371. Learn to juggle with three balls

4372. Drive the Autobahn

4373. Find a job you love

4374. Spend Christmas on the beach drinking piña coladas

4375. Overcome your fear of failure

4376. Raft through the Grand Canyon

4377. Donate money and put your name on something: a college scholarship, a bench in the park

4378. Buy your own house and then spend time making it into exactly what you want

4379. Grow a garden

4380. Spend three months getting your body into optimum shape

4381. Drive a convertible with the top down and music blaring

4382. Accept yourself for who you are

4383. Learn to use a microphone and give a speech in public

4384. Scuba dive off Australia's Great Barrier Reef

4385. Go up in a hot-air balloon

4386. Attend one really huge rock concert

4387. Kiss someone you've just met on a blind date

4388. Be able to handle: your tax forms, Jehovah's Witnesses, your banker, telephone solicitors

4389. Spend a winter at an Antarctica research station

4390. Lose more money than you can afford at roulette in Vegas

4391. Let someone feed you peeled, seedless grapes

4392. Kiss the Blarney stone and develop the gift of gab

4393. Fart in a crowded space

4394. Make love on the kitchen floor

4395. Go deep sea fishing and eat your catch

4396. Create your own website

4397. Visit the Holy Land

4398. Make yourself spend a half-day at a concentration camp and swear never to forget

4399. Run to the top of the Statue of Liberty

4400. Go on an Amazon rainforest tour

4401. Catch a ball in the stands of a major league baseball stadium

4402. Make a hole-in-one

4403. Ski a double-black diamond run

4404. Learn to bartend

4405. Run a marathon

4406. Look into your child's eyes, see yourself, and smile

4407. Reflect on your greatest weakness, and realize how it is your greatest strength

4408. Inspire someone

4409. Direct a short film

4410. Give Dad a new car

4411. Witness the *Aurora Borealis*

4412. Spend a year in a monastery/convent

Survive Disasters

4413. Be prepared for the worst

4414. Don't freeze up

4415. Practice reacting to emergency situations with family and friends and, if possible, your community

4416. Know that one person can make a difference

4417. Reach out to friends, family, and community

4418. As a family, discuss the role each member of family would play

4419. Be creative and innovative if required

4420. Sit down with your family and friends and create a list of survival necessities for all of you

4421. Stay calm—if you're calm, others are more likely to stay calm

4422. Endure through the aftermath—the aftermath can be as difficult as the disaster itself

4423. Know some basic rules and guidelines Information is available from many organizations, the library, the internet, etc.

4424. Complete a risk assessment before anything happens Natural threats vary by region. Hazard maps are available on FEMA's website

4425. When planning for disaster, consider the risk potential of your area. Example: if you live in a flood or earthquake zone, make sure your property is accordingly insured

4426. Keep a basic first-aid kit including bandages and medicine

4427. Stockpile butterfly bandages, gauze, and ace bandage

4428. Stockpile medicines, which should include an anti-inflammatory such as aspirin, an antihistamine, and diarrhea medicine

4429. Also stockpile a pair of rubber gloves, paramedic's scissors, alcohol pads, hand sanitizer, antibiotic ointment, duct tape, and a CPR face mask

4430. Use a small plastic container as a waterproof, cheap carrying case for the supplies

4431. Keep a first-aid kit in the car, which should include a 250-psi air compressor, a set of jumper cables, a reflective triangle. For winter breakdowns include a fleece hat, gloves and scarf and tundra sleeping bag

4432. Keep a pocket-sized first-aid kit for special situations. This should include a small moleskin pad for blisters, antiseptic and alcohol pads to clean wounds

4433. If you have a boat, keep a first-aid kit on the boat. This kit should include provisions for injuries common at sea, including aloe vera gel, nausea medication and information on hook removal

4434. Keep a nonhuman first-aid kit. This kit can include a skin staple gun that seals deep wounds, a pill gun to administer medicine, immunization records, and photo ID

4435. Keep a bottle of iodine; it is versatile

4436. Keep $300 cash in small denominations in your house. Without electricity, the ATM won't work and merchants won't take large bills

4437. Keep a backup set of eyeglasses

4438. Keep a battery-operated or crank radio

4439. Keep a radio that gives NOAA weather alerts

4440. Keep matches in waterproof bag or box

4441. Keep a supply of candles; often, after a few days, they turn out to be the light source

4442. Keep a fire extinguisher

4443. Buy a generator and learn how to safely operate it

4444. Store gasoline for the generator

4445. If you live in the country, consider a wood-burning stove with a large supply of wood for emergencies

4446. Keep a lightweight axe to cut firewood as source of heat

4447. Keep a supply of propane for cooking

4448. Have a way to cook your food in an emergency. This might include cans of sterno, a propane camping stove (with a few bottles of propane), or a small portable charcoal grill (use wood if charcoal is not available)

4449. Keep a compass and know how to use it. Many come with a built-in thermometer and signaling mirror

4450. Keep rope

4451. Keep heavy gloves for removing debris

4452. Keep a first-aid manual

4453. Keep tools that might be required such as chain saw, shovel, rake, hose, hatchet, knife, hammer, drill/driver, circular saw

4454. Keep fully powered backup batteries for the tools

4455. Buy more supplies than you need. Neighbors and friends may not have prepared as well as you have. They will also need food and water

4456. Keep a Bible. It may be the most important source of strength and courage for you and your family

4457. Important paperwork should be ready for rapid evacuation. This should include bank records, insurance policies, personal identification and medical records, and copies of deeds. Seal it all in a waterproof bag

4458. Maintain a copy of important documentation in three locations: a safe-deposit box, with a friend or family member in another location at least fifty miles away, and a quick-getaway bag (grab and go)

4459. Prepare a quick-getaway bag with the essentials and keep it by the front door. Include a prepaid phone card, flashlight, matches, batteries, food, flashlight, National Oceanic and Atmospheric Association (NOAA) weather radio, extra keys to house and car, prescription medications, $300 in small denominations

4460. Keep local maps and a road atlas in your car

4461. Keep writing supplies in your car

4462. Stockpile extra batteries for flashlight and radio and anything else you need

4463. Keep extra supplies of toilet paper and moist towelettes in car and home

4464. Keep backup sleeping bag and blankets in car

4465. Keep light sticks or roadside flares in the car

4466. Keep cell-phone charger in the car

4467. Keep a manual can opener. Remember, you'll be off the grid

4468. For those with infants, be sure you have a fourteen-day supply of pediatric medicines, disposable diapers, disposable cleansing clothes, formula (a mother's milk supply can be affected by shock, injury, or even death)

4469. In your emergency supply kit, don't forget walkers, dentures or special medical supplies for seniors

4470. Stockpile food. Always have at least 9600 calories worth of food available per person

4471. Days one and two after disaster, eat dairy products and meat, which last four hours in an unpowered refrigerator. Frozen food can last up to two days

4472. Check food in unpowered refrigerator with a meat thermometer; anything above 41° F should be thrown out

4473. Days three to seven after disaster, eat fruits and vegetables. Most fruit can last up to seven days at room temperature

4474. If you have potatoes when the disaster hits, move them to a cool, dark place and they should last over a week

4475. After seven days, eat food in jars and cans and packaged goods

4476. Keep a good supply of unopened peanut butter and jelly in the house; it can last up to a year unopened

4477. Considered long-term emergency rations such as ready-to-eat meals (MREs). Many are available for purchase on the Internet

4478. Always keep three days' supply of bottled water on hand. One person needs one gallon of clean drinkable water a day

4479. Keep water clean with a backup filter

4480. Keep several gallons of bleach in the house; it can be used to purify water

4481. If supply of water runs out, collect drinking water from home pipes. Close off the main water valve, open a top floor faucet, and then drain water through the faucet at the lowest point in your house

4482. Purify contaminated water collected from rain or streams or lakes by filtering it through a paper towel or clean cloth or coffee filter to remove particle. To sterilize the water, boil it or add 16 drops of household bleach per gallon and wait 30 minutes before consuming

4483. Keep a handheld CB radio. Find one that also tunes into NOAA weather channels

4484. Keep 3-mil contractor bags. They can take sharp debris and double as a poncho or water protection

4485. Keep glow bracelets and put them with essentials like flashlights and door handles. Without electricity, it gets dark fast

4486. Keep one or more lanterns in the house

4487. Practice operating emergency equipment with members of your family

4488. Keep "off the grid" entertainment such as games and puzzles

4489. Consider buying a small solar panel or wind turbine for off the grid backup

4490. A five-gallon plastic bucket which can be converted to a makeshift toilet

4491. Keep a metal bucket for cooking and boiling water

4492. Keep a clean trash can; it's waterproof and can be used to collect water

4493. Heavy-duty trash bags can be used to replace sleeping bags—they retain heat and repeal water

4494. Consider a power inverter for your car; it allows the cigarette-lighter jack to be used as an AC plug

4495. Keep a corded landline phone that does not rely on electricity

4496. Keep a plastic ripstop tarp at least 12 feet by 12 feet

4497. Keep a good-quality knife and multipurpose tool

4498. Keep bottles of hand sanitizer in your first-aid and emergency kits

4499. Never let your gas tank go below a quarter tank; if you know a disaster is coming, fill the tank

4500. If you know a disaster is coming, check and familiarize yourself with the evacuation route and possible alternatives in case the initial route is closed

4501. If you know a disaster is coming, contact relatives and friends to let them know your plans. Provide backup contact information

4502. If you know a disaster is coming, always have a primary plan and a backup plan including where you will go, how you will get there, and what you will take with you

4503. If you know a disaster is coming, be sure you have a month's supply of medication on hand. Pharmacies may not be open for some time

4504. Keep a written card on yourself and each member of your family containing a list of family and emergency (doctor, etc.) contacts. If you rely on a cell phone contact list and the battery runs down, you may not be able to recharge the phone, and you will have no numbers

4505. Set up a point person at least fifty miles away, in case all local telecommunications fail

4506. Make sure all members of the family and friends have the number of the point person. Even if family members or friends can't reach each other, they can get vital information through the point person

4507. Work with your community to make sure at least two local gas stations have power backup generators so they can provide gasoline off the grid

4508. Work with your community to identify people who might need special protection such as the elderly or handicapped

4509. Work with your community to establish a central emergency help area

4510. Keep a simple wrench available to shut off gas and water valves. Emergency tools are now available to handle these valves easily and with one tool

4511. If you have important information on your computer, keep it backed up in a location at least fifty miles from where you live. Or put it on a jump drive and have a trusted friend or family member keep it if they live at least fifty miles away

4512. Consider an LED flashlight; batteries can last ten times longer in an LED flashlight. LEDs have no fragile parts and can withstand shock much better than a regular flashlight

Earthquake

4513. If you live in an earthquake zone, keep a pair of sturdy, comfortable shoes next to the bed so you can slip them on quickly

4514. If you have children, have the children keep flashlights under their pillows

4515. Keep a flashlight next to the bed

4516. Stage emergency drills with your family and friends

4517. Crawl under a sturdy table and cover your face and head with your arms

4518. Stay away from windows and large bureaus and things that might fall

4519. Leave the building immediately after the shaking stops. Aftershock may soon follow and bring down more structures

4520. If you're outside, avoid buildings and utility wires

4521. If you're trapped under debris, cover your mouth with a cloth or shirt

4522. If you're trapped under debris, tap against a pipe or any object that will make noise

4523. If you're trapped under debris, don't yell for help unless you have to because you risk inhaling dangerous quantities of dust or hazardous materials

4524. After an earthquake, do not light a match or candle because there might be a gas leak

4525. After the earthquake, find a safe location

4526. After the earthquake, get to your car if it's safe. In the car, you should have a flashlight, two blankets, first-aid kit, hand sanitizer, and radio

4527. After the earthquake, immediately help anybody who has been hurt. Control bleeding and keep wounds clean

4528. After the earthquake, listen to the radio for emergency information

4529. After the earthquake, do not make phone calls for the first hour unless it's an emergency. This will allow the lines to stay open for real emergencies

4530. After the earthquake and once you're sure the shaking has stopped, move your car out of the garage and away from power lines and structures

4531. After the earthquake, remove heavy items from high shelves and place fragile items on floor

4532. Trust your common sense

Flood

4533. If there's a flash-flood warning, immediately move to higher ground—don't waste time gathering your possessions

4534. If flooding is predicted, turn off your electricity and water. (Shut off natural gas only if authorities so advise)

4535. If you have time to evacuate before a flood, move valuable and essential items to higher elevations (upstairs, etc.)

4536. Remember, if you have time to evacuate before a flood, do not jeopardize the lives of yourself or family or friends. Getting out is the most important task; don't assume you have more time than you do

4537. Avoid downed powerlines

4538. Stay out of moving water. Six inches of moving water can make you fall; a foot will float most cars

4539. Don't touch electrical equipment while wet or standing in water

4540. If you live in a flood zone, go over emergency procedures and behavior with your family and/or friends. Knowing what you're going to do can save your life and the lives of those you love

Tornado

4541. If you hear a storm warning, tune to an NOAA weather radio for tornado alerts

4542. Know the warning signs of a tornado: darkening skies with a sickly greenish color or an orange color; strong persistent rotation of the cloud base; extreme calm and quiet during or right after the thunderstorm; a rumble or roar that sounds like continuous thunder or a train

4543. A warning sign for a tornado at night is the blue-green or white flashes at ground level in the distance, which is power lines being snapped by high wind

4544. If you're under a tornado warning and/or see or hear an approaching tornado or note any of the signs, go immediately to your basement

4545. If you have no basement, go to a storm shelter, neighbor's basement, or the lowest floor of your structure. Avoid corners, windows, and doors

4546. Do not open windows

4547. Get under a sturdy table and protect your head with your arms

4548. Only grab clothes and shoes if you have the time

4549. If you're in your car, get out and seek shelter, even if your best choice is in the nearest ditch, depression, or flat outdoor location. Close your eyes and cover your head with your arms

4550. If the tornado hits, cover your eyes. Tornadoes can drive specks of dust into the eyeballs

4551. If you live in tornado country, practice an emergency routine with your family and/or friends . A tornado often allows only seconds; know exactly what you're going to do and how to do it

Hurricane

4552. In case of an approaching hurricane, bring outside possessions into the house or securely tie them down

4553. Board your windows

4554. If flooding is also probable, move furniture and movable objects to the upper floor of your house. Disconnect any electrical appliances that can't be moved

4555. Do not stack sandbags around the outside walls of your house to keep water out of the basement. Water might seeps through the earth and collect around the basement walls and under the floor, severely damaging the house

4556. If you're told to evacuate, evacuate. Riding out a hurricane is a dangerous and unpredictable choice Is any material object worth your life or the lives of those you love?

4557. If you have not been told to evacuate, stay inside. Don't try to travel because you risk injury from flying debris, downed wires, and flooded roads

4558. Know your evacuation route and alternative routes

4559. Monitor the news stations for the best routes out

4560. In case of a hurricane, secure and brace external doors

4561. Close all interior doors

4562. Take refuge in a small interior room, hallway, or closet on the lowest level of your home

4563. Lie on the floor under a table or sturdy piece of furniture

4564. Keep your curtains and blinds closed

4565. Stay away from the windows even if there is a lull and the winds seem to be dying—it could be the passing eye of the hurricane and winds will soon pick back up

4566. If you live in a hurricane zone, practice emergency procedures with your friends and family

Thunderstorm

4567. If a severe thunderstorm approaches, get inside a house, building, or hardtop vehicle

4568. Shutter windows and secure outside doors; close curtains

4569. Use a corded phone for emergencies. Cordless and cell phones are not reliable

4570. Unplug appliances; power surges can cause severe damage

4571. If you're outside, avoid tall, isolated trees which attract lightning

4572. If you're outside, seek shelter in a low area under a thick growth of small trees. If you're on open water, get to land and seek shelter immediately

Fire

4573. Get a smoke alarm and place on in every bedroom and on every story. Change batteries twice a year

4574. Keep at least one fire extinguisher on each story

4575. Put a folding escape ladder in every bedroom above the first floor

4576. Practice home fire escape with your family. Discuss your escape plan, and practice turning off the thermostat while blindfolded

4577. If a fire starts, check the door. If it's hot, step away. If the door is open and you see smoke or fire, close it

4578. If a fire starts, block the smoke by using blankets or towels to cover the bottom of the door

4579. In a fire, get low. Near the ground the temperature is much cooler and there's less smoke

4580. Crawl to the window while staying low. Open the window. If you're on the first or second floor, jump. If you're higher, crouch below the windowsill and wait—it's the first place rescuers will look for you

Natural Disaster

4581. After a natural disaster, look for injured people and do what you can to help. Use common sense in terms of those you can help and those you can't

4582. Stay away from your house if powerlines are touching it

4583. Stay away from your house if you smell gas

4584. Stay away from your house if it appears to be leaning or if the structure has detached from its foundation

4585. Shut off the main circuit breaker if you suspect damage to the house's internal wiring. Do not attempt this if the electrical panel is covered with water

4586. Snap pictures and take notes for an insurance claim

4587. Call your insurance company and schedule an inspection from an adjuster

4588. Survey your property for problems that require immediate attention

4589. Make only emergency repairs such as plugging holes in the roof or covering doors and windows with tarp or plastic sheeting

4590. Hold off on other repairs until the adjuster arrives

4591. Check on your neighbors

4592. Clear away broken glass and dangerous debris

4593. Remove sodden materials such as carpeting or drywall before mold develops

4594. Keep a positive outlook. The right outlook will help you and all those around you more than you can imagine

4595. Reach out to your friends, family, and community. Together you can rebuild

Build a Better Church

4596. Buy church cookbooks. They always contain the best recipes

4597. Talk openly about money and faithfulness to God

4598. Model the giving spirit you seek from your fellow members in your church

4599. Reinforce giving as an act of worship

4600. Volunteer your services to the church and the church community

4601. Ask your pastor if someone on your church's sick list would like a visit, then visit her

4602. Create a Jubilee Fund in your church congregation, matching every dollar you spend internally with a dollar externally. If you have a building fund, create a fund to match it to give away and buy mosquito nets or dig wells for folks dying in poverty

4603. Visit a worship service where you will be a minority. Invite someone to dinner at your house and have dinner with someone at their home if they invite you

4604. Help your church create a Peacemaker Scholarship and give it to a young person trying to avoid the economic draft—who would like to go to college but sees no other way than through the military

4605. Confess something you have done wrong, and ask for forgiveness

4606. Start a quilt or knitting ministry

4607. Pick up the extra bulletins after service and put them in their appropriate places

4608. Put kneelers up after Mass

4609. Sit in the first pew

4610. Writer a thank you note to the organist and other lay volunteers

4611. Volunteer to clean the church before the holidays and after

4612. Pick someone up who can't drive to attend church services on a regular basis

4613. Help out with Sunday School

4614. Organize a prayer chain

4615. Attend and spend at church fundraisers

4616. Volunteer to serve at a fish fry

4617. Stuff church mailings

4618. Volunteer to help with funeral meals

4619. Learn the story of a foreign missionary

4620. Sign up for a Bible-study course at your church

4621. Commit to reading one book on spirituality during Christmas/Easter/Passover

4622. Attend church regularly

Christmas Journey

4623. Gather your family every evening and read aloud an Advent devotion

4624. Instead of using pretty Christmas wrapping paper, wrap your gifts in decorated brown paper grocery bags, shopping ads and the funnies section of the newspaper

4625. Let somebody else go in front of you in a busy line at the checkout counter even though she seems agitated and grumpy

4626. Randomly give grocery gift cards to people in a grocery store in a less-desirable area of town

4627. Before you wrap presents for your own children, gather gently used toys and bring to a women's shelter

4628. Gather friends and family, sing Christmas carols to your local firefighters on Christmas Eve, and leave them with plenty of Christmas cookies

4629. Have your children design and decorate Christmas cards and deliver them to a local nursing home

4630. Collect used coats in your neighborhood and deliver to a local homeless shelter

4631. Instead of walking by the shopping cart in the corral in the parking lot, bring the cart you'll need inside in with you

4632. Buy a Christmas tree for someone who might need one

4633. Invite a neighbor or a neighbor's family to join you for Christmas Eve or Christmas Day even if you don't know him very well but know he is new in town

4634. Purchase a poinsettia for your church's Christmas services and ask your church to give it to a homebound person after services

4635. Forgive someone and invite her into your Christmas

4636. Take a day off of household and holiday chores to enjoy the season

4637. Find unusual ways to serve others

4638. Start a new family tradition

4639. Introduce yourself to a neighbor you do not know

4640. Apologize and seek forgiveness

4641. Downsize the holiday season

4642. Give yourself the gift of peace of mind

4643. Hit the after-Christmas sales for others, not yourself

4644. Grieve with someone

4645. Drink lots of hot chocolate and little alcohol

4646. Let someone cut in front of you in line

4647. Be patient with clerks, customer service people, etc.

4648. Invite someone home who has no other place to go

4649. Form a "singles" family dinner for all the singles in your life

4650. Say a prayer of gratitude

4651. Memorize all the verses of a Christmas carol

4652. Go caroling

4653. Gather stockings and fill them with homemade goodies

4654. Make a nativity set from clay

4655. Hold a neighborhood *posadas* event

4656. Focus on feelings, not on material things

4657. Consider a homemade Christmas for the whole family

4658. Make tree ornaments with the kids

4659. Go sledding

4660. Make a holiday scrapbook for the family

4661. Watch *White Christmas, Miracle on 34th Street,* and *A Christmas Story*

4662. Read "A Visit from St. Nicholas ('Twas the Night Before Christmas")" to your kids on Christmas Eve

4663. Go to midnight church services

4664. Volunteer to be a Salvation Army bell ringer

4665. Write letters to Santa

4666. Spend time reflecting on the last year and on expectations for the new year

4667. Don't spend yourself into debt

Lenten Journey

4668. Turn the other cheek—the temptation for revenge is always there, but don't give in!

4669. Pray before every meal, remembering to give thanks. It might seem trite, but it's a habit that is hard to break once you've started. And don't give that up just because you are at a restaurant

4670. Next time you hear somebody gossiping, politely tell them you used to gossip, but you've decided not to do that anymore

4671. Instead of giving up something for Lent, give for Lent

4672. Invite a friend to join you in daily Lenten devotions. Even if your friend is far away, you can discuss the devotion via Facebook or instant messaging

4673. Text a simple love message to your special someone twice a day—don't expect a text back, but do it twice a day for the whole season

4674. Fast for Lent

4675. Follow the tradition of no meat on Fridays

4676. Buy nothing new during the Lenten season

4677. Join in eucharistic adoration

4678. Be faithful to your Lenten promises

4679. Make Lent a time of self-improvement and transformation

4680. Begin with Ash Wednesday services

4681. Buy an Easter lily for your home

4682. Adopt the European tradition of collecting bells you have to ring on Sundays of the Lent

4683. Make your Lenten sacrifice something important to you

4684. Sing the hymn "O Sacred Heart"

4685. Explain the word *redemption* to a child

4686. Celebrate the resurrection

4687. Read Exodus 12:1-42 to children

4688. Volunteer for projects that help the poorest and most abandoned

4689. Remember to say grace at mealtime

4690. Pray the rosary as a family

4691. Discuss the meaning of the Lenten tradition

4692. Participate in Operation Rice Bowl (www.crs.org)

Creating Miracles

4693. Hold the highest vision—look at all the possibilities and what could be

4694. Obliterate problems and invite miracles—open your heart and mind to allow miracles to happen

4695. Insulate yourself from toxic influences—limit exposure to negativity

4696. Each day choose between thoughts and feelings that add to your energy or deplete it

4697. Remember that fear gets you nowhere—it is detrimental to your physical health too

4698. Practice forgiveness

4699. Give thanks every day

Improve Communication Skills

4700. People hear what they see

4701. People want to know what's in it for them—so tell them

4702. Recognize that people of all types are motivated by the same things

4703. Know what you want to say to people—practice if necessary

4704. Control fear

4705. Stop talking and listen

4706. Believe in your message

4707. Repeat major points

4708. Understand what your audience wants—whether it is one person or a roomful

4709. Don't use acronyms

4710. Reduce jargon

4711. Humor is good

4712. Illustrate what you have to say with anecdotes and stories

4713. Ask for questions and feedback

4714. Enunciate and project (remember high school drama class)

4715. Practice pronouncing names, terms, and really big words

4716. Make eye contact—you are trying to get through to people

4717. Don't stand like a statue—use your body and hands

4718. Talk like a person, not a robot

4719. Be prepared to stop and listen

4720. Concentrate on the message, not the words

4721. Ask questions if you are in the audience

4722. Ask questions if you are the presenter

4723. Accept complaints

4724. Get to the point

4725. Ask for what you want

4726. Use active verbs

4727. Use gender-neutral language (don't man the booth, staff it)

4728. If using statistics, cite your sources

4729. Express emotions—tell people why they should join you in this passion for doing good

4730. Keep It Simple, Stupid (KISS it)

4731. Paint a picture

4732. Support your statements with data and recognized or certified authorities

4733. Keep in mind you are here to improve things

4734. Visualize all the possibilities

4735. Be flexible

4736. Be likable

4737. Commit yourself to the desired results

4738. Empathize with those who will be impacted

4739. Don't take yourself too seriously

4740. Eliminate your internal negative feelings

4741. The best idea should win regardless of whose it is. Be receptive to changing your plan to a better plan of someone else's

4742. Take responsibility—not just credit

4743. Respect the impact of stress on the communications process

4744. Be real

4745. Check your ego at the door

4746. Recognize manipulative behavior

4747. Recognize condescending manners

4748. Avoid hard and hurtful words—remember, you are trying to communicate ideas

4749. Handle disagreements with tact—everyone has a point

4750. Don't waste time

4751. Plan productive meetings

4752. Consider the experience level of those involved

4753. Time and timing is everything

4754. Keep up on current events

4755. Keep up on the needs of others

4756. Read something inspirational

4757. Do your research

Lead the Charge to Paradise

4758. Courage is not a one-time event

4759. Don't just think big, think gargantuan

4760. Timing is everything, but timing can be created

4761. Lead fearlessly especially when you're scared to death

4762. Volunteer to help before you even know what the project is

4763. Show up early for meetings and welcome everyone

4764. Be willing to facilitate a meeting for someone else

4765. Prepare for meetings, don't just show up

4766. Understand meetings should not be your only form of communication

4767. Always treat others with respect

4768. Be transparent and share personal stories

4769. Provide regular feedback about behaviors and actions

4770. Share your vision

4771. Accept that others have visions, too

4772. Make special note of skills you see in your team

4773. Start a network with others outside your circle who have common issues

4774. Develop and use consistent positive feedback

4775. Admit mistakes

4776. Display or publish your personal values

4777. Share with others your vulnerabilities

4778. Make proactive calls to maintain your network

4779. Keep performance and expectations independent of any personal relationship

4780. Communicate clearly

4781. Spend time communicating one-on-one with others

4782. Ask about others' motives

4783. Start informal learning time at lunch with colleagues

4784. Use email to spread information

4785. Share new skills

4786. Offer to assist in the learning process

4787. Put at least one thing into action on a regular basis

4788. Show empathy and compassion to others

4789. Find a mentor to focus your own development

4790. Mentor someone else

4791. Actively pursue and encourage continuous improvements for yourself and others

4792. Continue to grow and raise your expectations over time

4793. Follow the example of leaders you admire

4794. Encourage and promote change

4795. Be enthusiastic and passionate

4796. Say no to unimportant requests

4797. Bring up and engage in a difficult subject or conversations

4798. Keep your actions and decisions aligned with your values

4799. Listen more than you talk

4800. Be bold in your actions

4801. Tackle your biggest fear by facing it head-on

4802. Be persistent

4803. Maintain your personal ethics

4804. Be confident in your abilities and decisions

4805. Strengthen your unique attributes

4806. Do what you say and carry through on your commitment

4807. Work hard, play hard

4808. Maintain a sense of balance

4809. Let go of perfectionism for yourself and others

4810. Take risks! Take more risks!

4811. Take the initiative

4812. Eliminate distractions

4813. Set time for personal strategic planning

4814. Review your accomplishments

4815. Remember you are a servant leader

4816. Always give credit to those you work with and who work for you

4817. Admit and accept fault

4818. Don't let previous failures define your successes

4819. Be open-minded to cultural differences

4820. Stay calm

4821. Control emotional outbreaks

4822. Sacrifice your time and personal goals to achieve the goals of the collective

4823. Take on tasks no one else will accept

4824. Find your own passions

4825. Connect with others in the community who share those passions

4826. Use the 5 W's (who, what, when, where, and why)

4827. Keep complacency at bay

4828. Drive through the resistance of others

4829. Let go of having things done your way

4830. Seek alternative pathways

4831. Put love into what you do and how you do it

4832. Build trust by trusting people before they've earned it

4833. Rely on and reveal your spiritual guidance

4834. Make decisions that build teams

4835. Do the right thing, even if it won't be popular

4836. Give first without expectations

4837. Be willing to serve others

Improving Life When You Don't Have a Job

4838. Check out the free-admission days at museums and zoos in your area

4839. Start a blog

4840. Update your profile on Linked In (www.linkedin.com)

4841. Spend more time with your family

4842. Volunteer at your church

4843. Exercise and keep your mind fresh

4844. Catch up on your reading through your local library

4845. Go back to school and finish your degree

4846. Take advantage of retraining programs and change careers

4847. Return to an old hobby

4848. Pick up a new hobby

4849. Plan time to network online each day

4850. Don't like where the world is going?—become politically active

4851. Study philosophy—what is the meaning of life?

4852. Take free course through MIT (ocw.mit.edu)

4853. Explore your own environment with a walk each day to a new area

4854. Become a mentor at your local YMCA or through Big Brothers/Big Sisters

4855. Find old friends online and begin networking with them

4856. Reorganize your closets

4857. Volunteer for a mission trip with your church

4858. Volunteer at the library

4859. Go to job fairs

4860. Start gardening (especially vegetable gardening)

4861. Volunteer at the animal shelter

4862. Join the Peace Corps or AmeriCorps

4863. Take up roller skating

4864. Train to become a volunteer firefighter or emergency medical technician

4865. Play board games with your spouse

4866. Clean out your car—clean out your spouse's car

4867. Visit with neighbors

4868. Visit seniors at a nursing home

4869. Spend more time with your kids

4870. Spend more time with your pets

4871. Keep an absolutely immaculate yard

4872. Limit your television time

4873. Make peace with someone from your past

4874. Learn to play tennis

4875. Begin the practice of daily meditation

4876. Start a band

4877. See if you can sit in on college classes that interest you

4878. Join the local theater company

4879. Take up low-cost cooking for your whole family

4880. Join the choir

4881. Volunteer at a homeless or women's shelter

4882. Research your family tree

4883. Walk the neighbor's dog

4884. Begin scrapbooking and get your family photos in order

4885. Explore You Tube (www.youtube.com)

4886. Set up your profile and resumé on various job-search websites

4887. Take a painting class

4888. Take a writing class

4889. Join a job seekers support group

4890. Create your own videos for You Tube

4891. Build your own website

4892. Learn to dance

4893. Go swimming

4894. Make a list of all the things you can do for free, and then do at least three a week

4895. Make a list of your goals—and a plan to reach them

4896. Embrace your inner child—but don't forget your outer adult

4897. Keep a journal of what you do each day

4898. Help friends with babysitting

4899. Become a chess champ

4900. Begin recycling and freecycling

4901. Clean the house

4902. Perform a maintenance survey of your house—take free classes at home-improvement stores and make the repairs yourself

4903. Do interview role-playing with other job seekers

4904. Clean out your home-computer files

4905. Take computer-maintenance classes

4906. Write down the pros and cons of your previous jobs

4907. Define what you "need" from a new job

4908. Attend local lectures in your community—most are free

4909. Write an editorial for your local paper

4910. Take the time to talk to your family—all of them

4911. Leave the car at home and take public transportation

4912. Pull out that old telescope and refresh your astronomy knowledge

4913. Don't feel guilty for having a little fun—and don't let anyone else make you feel guilty about it either

4914. Listen to yourself

Setting Goals That Change Lives

4915. Brainstorm with yourself and others

4916. Set a realistic, but challenging/inspiring goal

4917. Analyze your needs

4918. Define and describe your goals in great detail

4919. Plan ahead—look at how the actions of working on the goal impact your work, family and time

4920. Ask your family and close friends for input—your goals may impact them

4921. Make a list of your personal strengths in relationship to your goal

4922. Research the various aspects of your goal

4923. Commit to time to work toward your goal

4924. Commit to a deadline

4925. Don't be a one-trick pony—working on goals should not exclude other aspects of your life

4926. Break it down into tasks

4927. Keep it visible and visual

4928. Figure out a step-by-step plan

4929. Acquire good project-management tools and skills

4930. Listen to your internal dialogue

4931. Create benchmarks or milestones

4932. Check your progress regularly

4933. Revisit, reevaluate, and if necessary, adjust your goals

4934. Do not skip steps needed to achieve the goal

4935. Remember, in problem-solving, spend 20% of your time thinking about the problem and 80% of your time thinking about the solution

4936. Remind yourself that you will achieve your goals

4937. Ask friends and family to be part of the process or join you on the journey

4938. Keep stakeholders informed of progress

4939. Be realistic about when to give in

Create a Personal Mission Statement

4940. Confront work problems full-tilt boogie

4941. It's not just what you say, but the time and place you say it

4942. Change doesn't have an end—the risk is in creating the first change

4943. Make the important decisions when you're emotionally balanced

4944. You can learn something from everyone—even the biggest of jerks

4945. Seek your life's purpose—consider using the Zen form of self-investigation

4946. Define your life's purpose—or at least your perceived purpose

4947. Keep it short, simple, and memorable—sometimes even one sentence will do

4948. It should be the guiding principle of what you want to become—in the short-term and long-term

4949. It should be positive

4950. It should be realistic

4951. Commit to your mission statement with love and compassion

4952. It should be communal

4953. Money has no place in this mission statement—this isn't about achieving practical goals, but about the kind of person you want to be at your very core

4954. It must be part of your everyday life—a day-to-day positive guide

4955. Ensure your mission statement fits with all areas of your life

4956. It should be balanced—for you and for those in your life

4957. Ask yourself, "Can I passionately embrace this?"—if not, it's not for you

4958. Do others recognize you in the statement itself?

4959. Be yourself—just a much better self

4960. Reevaluate your statement at least twice a year

4961. Seek continuous improvement

4962. Remember that this is not a goal, but a statement of mission

Taking Risks

4963. Understand that there is no such thing as a risk-free life

4964. Understand the risks you are taking

4965. Look at how you will manage the risk

4966. Analyze the downside and decide whether you're willing to live with it

4967. Determine whether the size of the risk is proportionate to the success of the outcome

4968. Create a fall-back plan

4969. Contain the damage to yourself and others

4970. Consider all the options before jumping in

4971. Create a checklist for risks—analyze the key components

4972. If the risk outcome impacts other people, keep them informed or ask permission

4973. Be results-oriented

4974. Cultivate an attitude of optimism

4975. Cultivate empathy

4976. Improve your decision-making abilities by learning from your failures as well as your successes

4977. Accept responsibility for your actions

4978. Take only purposeful risks

4979. Don't be intimidated by risk factors

4980. See the big picture—or at least the bigger picture

4981. Be flexible—be willing to change your mind

4982. Stand up for yourself

4983. Stand up for what is right

4984. Look beyond the immediate outcome to longer range implications

4985. Challenge yourself to find safer solutions that will reap the same benefits

4986. Be motivated

4987. Procrastination is fundamentally detrimental to you and the situation

4988. Make the stress of risk-taking an ally—let stress work as a red flag to tell you to take action

4989. Don't let risk-taking become addictive

4990. Don't let risk-taking stress work against you

Stayin' Alive

4991. Find a pay-it-forward activity you absolutely love

4992. Write a personal mission statement and live by it

4993. Define a way to hold yourself accountable

4994. Execute your plans to reach your goals—while having fun

4995. Eat well, sleep well, laugh often, and be yourself

4996. Remember, age is not a factor

4997. Be unpredictable

4998. Keep your sense of humor and sense of purpose

4999. Explore the world

5000. Just Do It—participate, participate, participate

And Finally ...

5001. Live every day as if it is your last...it just might be!